Old Testament 101

Daily Readings with study questions

by Jodi Green

Copyright 2016

By Jodi Green

All scripture quotations are from the New King James version.

Special Thanks

A special thank you to
Karissa Sherwin
who journeyed with me
through each lesson
for two years,
offering comments and suggestions
along the way.
You are a great blessing, Karissa!

Also, special thanks to my brother,
Jay Pettit
For his wonderful advice
and support throughout
this project
and my entire life.
I love you!

How to Use This Book

Old Testament 101 is a guide to studying the Old Testament in chronological order by reading one chapter per day, five days per week. This study is suitable for all ages, from middle school through adults.

There is great benefit in studying the Bible in an orderly way, as opposed to a random passage each day or even a needs-based study (for example, helping you through a particularly difficult situation). If you learn to study the Bible in a sequential way, you will eventually find what God's Word says about every conceivable human situation.

In this study you will have five days of readings each week, reading usually one chapter per day. This leaves the weekends to catch up on anything that was missed during the week. This study is a comprehensive overview in which some books have representative chapters chosen for continuity, while others will be studied in their entirety. In other words, not every chapter of the Old Testament is included for specific study, but I would encourage you to read all of them if you can. In the cases of events repeated in different books, usually only one account is studied.

Each lesson begins with an overview of the week's readings. Sometimes there are questions to consider in the overview that will help your general understanding of the lesson for that week. You may skip the overview, but it can be very beneficial to your understanding of the chapters for the week.

The questions are very straightforward and are designed to be answered in the simplest way. The primary goal is an understanding of God's Word rather than a specific application to your particular circumstances. Practice letting the Holy Spirit apply your day's reading as you meditate throughout the day on what His Word says.

On the "For Further Study" pages, there is a selected key verse(s) to think about, and blank lines in which you may write a prayer, other passages that stand out to you, or some other aspect of the study that you may want to remember.

If you are confused by any of the passages that you read, there are many available resources for answering your questions. I would encourage everyone who wants to study the Bible to find a Bible-believing church and become involved. The Holy Spirit is your best resource for understanding God's Word, but it is vital that your church leaders help you as well. There are many online helps, such as biblos.com and others listed in the "Study Helps" section in the back. Finding a mentor to help you can also be of great benefit.

May God bless you as you seek to know Him more through the study of His Word.

In Christ,

Jodi Green

"For the Word of God is living and powerful, and sharper than any two-edged sword, piercing even to the division of soul and spirit, and of joints and marrow, and is a discerner of the thoughts and intents of the heart." (Hebrews 4:12)

Lesson 1

Overview

What a person believes about Genesis forms the basis for what he or she believes about everything. For example: do you really believe the Biblical account of creation, the entrance of sin and the flood? Do you really believe Abraham's family is God's chosen people? As you read and study Genesis, you will have the opportunity to think about what you really believe about the Bible. Will you be among the majority and decide that only parts of the Bible are true? Will you pick out for yourself which parts are true and which parts are not? Will you trust modern scientists and social engineers over God's Word? Is the Bible really God's Word? Is it true? Or does science prove the Genesis account is incorrect?

As you think about these questions, it would be of great benefit to spend some time in research about the claims of modern science concerning the origin of the universe and evolution. Some helpful places to begin are: www.answersingenesis.org; www.icr.org; www.creationtoday.org.

So now, it's time to dig in to the first 5 chapters. These chapters make up so much of the basis of what to believe about the rest of the Bible that it will be helpful to spend at least two weeks reading and studying them. Get in the habit of reading slowly and carefully. Think through exactly what God is telling you in each verse. There is so much controversy, even among Christians, over these beginnings. Answer the questions thoughtfully. Chapter 1 gives the creation overview, while chapter 2 fills in some greater detail. Chapter 3 shows the beginning of sin. If there are notes in your Bible, form the habit of cross-referencing. For example, Genesis does not give us the origin of the devil, but Ezekiel 28:11-19 explains a lot of what we know about him.

Lesson 1

Daily Bible Study

Day 1: Read Genesis 1

How and when did God create light? (v. 1-5)

What did God make on the second and third days? (v. 6-13)

What did God make on the fourth and fifth days? (v. 14-23)

What did God make on the sixth day? (v. 24-31)

Beginning in verse 11, count the number of times the phrase, "according to its kind" (or the equivalent in your translation) is repeated: _____ What does this phrase mean?

Day 2: Read Genesis 2

What did God do on the seventh day, and how did He describe it? (v. 1-3)

How did man receive life? (v. 4-7)

Where exactly was the garden? (v. 8-14)

What restrictions and warnings did God give? (v. 15-17)

How did God make the first woman and why? (v. 18-25)

Day 3: Read Genesis 3

What were the serpent's first words to the woman? (v. 1)

How did she change God's words? (v. 2-3)

Why did she eat the fruit? (v. 4-6)

Why did they hide? (v. 7-13)

What were the results? (v. 14-19)

How did God clothe them and why? (v. 20-24)

Day 4: Read Genesis 4

What was the difference in the offerings? (v. 1-5)

How did Cain respond? (v. 6-10)

What was the result? (v. 11-16)

Describe Cain's life and family. (v. 17-24)

How was Seth's family different from Cain's? (v. 25-26)

Day 5: Read Genesis 5

Why do you think these birth and death records are so precise? (v. 1-20)

What happened with Enoch and why? (v. 21-24)

What was the relationship of Methuselah and Noah? (v. 25-32)

For Further Study

Key Verse: "In the beginning God created the heavens and the earth."

Genesis 1:1

(This page is designed for you to write anything else that stood out to you in your Bible study or questions you may have. Also, writing out memory work is helpful. You may also use this space for sermon notes.)

Lesson 2

Overview

The story of Noah and the ark is one of the most popular stories in the entire Bible. In fact, almost every culture on our planet has a great flood story in its history, even the ones who do not know the Bible. So, are we meant to believe this story is real? That it actually happened? Is there anything at all to suggest that the story is a parable or an allegory? How do we know if these people are real or imaginary? As you read and study the Bible, form the habit of letting the Bible explain itself to you. For example, to determine whether a story is real or a parable, find an example that you know is a parable, and see how it is introduced. Look up the Good Samaritan story (Luke 10:30-37). Does it seem to be told as a historical fact or as a parable?

It should be clear that the Bible presents the account of the flood as a factual part of history. If you spend some time on the websites mentioned in Lesson 1, you will find a great amount of scientific evidence that shows the truth of this account.

There are parts to this story that hold mystery for us. For example, in chapter 6, who exactly were the sons of God and the daughters of men? Why were their children giants? Some scholars believe that the contrast was between Seth's descendants, who loved God, and Cain's descendants, who did not love God. The Bible doesn't tell us the answer. But we must develop the habit of trusting God to reveal to us what we need to know to understand His message of salvation to us. If there is something confusing, simply trust Him to show you what you need to know at the proper time. Just be sure you are getting all your facts from God's Word.

These chapters are also a good place to spend a couple of weeks reading and rereading in order to gain a deeper understanding.

Lesson 2

Daily Bible Study

Day 1: Read Genesis 6

What specifically grieved the Lord? (v. 1-6)
_____
_____

What specific sins are mentioned? (v. 7-12)
_____
_____

What shape was the ark? (v. 13-17)
_____

What did Noah do? (v. 18-22)
_____

Day 2: Read Genesis 7

How many of each kind of animal did Noah take? (v. 1-3)
_____

Describe where the flood waters came from. (v. 4-11)
_____

How high did the flood waters rise? (v. 12-20)
_____

How long did it rain (v. 17), and by verse 24 how long had they been in the ark? (v. 21-24)
_____
_____

Day 3: Read Genesis 8

How long had they been in the ark when the tops of the mountains became visible? (v. 1-5)
_____

How did Noah know the waters had receded? (v. 6-11)
_____
_____

How did Noah know when to leave the ark? (v. 12-19)

_____

Compare 8:14 to 7:11. How long were they in the ark total?

_____

What promise did God make? (v. 20-22)

_____

Day 4: Read Genesis 9

What do these verses imply about their eating habits? (v. 1-3)

_____

Why did God institute capital punishment? (v. 4-6)

_____

What is the significance of the rainbow? (v. 7-17)

_____

Why was Ham cursed while Shem and Japheth were blessed? (v. 18-29)

_____

Day 5: Read Genesis 10

Who is referred to in these verses and how are they described? (v. 1-5)

_____

Name several famous cities associated with Ham's family. (v. 6-20)

_____

Are any sons of Shem familiar to you? (v. 21-32)

_____

For Further Study

Key Verse: "But Noah found grace in the eyes of the Lord."
Genesis 6:8

Lesson 3

Overview

This week's reading begins with the famous story of the tower of Babel. In chapter 10 we read about the descendants of Noah and where they settled in ancient Mesopotamia. Verses 5, 20 and 31 mention the different languages. Chapter 11 goes back and fills in details about how the different languages came to be (similar to Genesis 2 which fills in details about chapter 1).

Something to think about: who was writing this history of the world? The first five books of the Old Testament are known as the Pentateuch and are attributed to Moses in several places in the Bible. Of course we think about 2 Timothy 3:16, "All scripture is given by inspiration of God...", but we also know that God chose human writers to pen the words He gave them (1 Peter 1:19-21). Genesis 5 and 10 begin with, "Now this is the genealogy of..." and that phrase appears twice in chapter 11. So did God supernaturally give Moses all the names and dates in Genesis? Or did Adam and Noah keep careful records that were preserved for those generations? Do you think Adam had a written language? Or do you picture Adam as a caveman drawing stick figures on cave walls? Though cavemen are not specifically mentioned in the Bible, it seems safe to assume that Adam and his sons were not cavemen. The most plausible place for cavemen in the Bible is here in chapter 11 when God confused their language, and they were forced to spread out as God had already told them to do.

Chapter 12 begins the account of God's covenant with Abraham and His own chosen people. Consider carefully the promises made to Abraham, especially in light of the on-going strife in that land to this very day. The sons of Abraham are still fighting over this all these many years later. We will see the beginning of the controversy as we study this section.

Lesson 3

Daily Bible Study

Day 1: Read Genesis 11

What were they building and why? (v. 1-4)
_____
_____

What was God's response? (v. 5-9)
_____
_____

How old was Shem during the flood? (v. 11-27)
_____

What is interesting about Terah? (v. 27-32)
_____
_____

Day 2: Read Genesis 12

What stands out to you about God's promises to Abram? (v. 1-3)
_____
_____

What do you think verse 3 means?
_____
_____

Where did Abram go, and what did God say about it? (v. 4-7)
_____
_____

Where exactly did Abram build this altar? (v. 8-9 – this place will be interesting in later study)
_____

Why did Abram lie, and how did God protect Sarai? (v. 10-20)
_____
_____

Day 3: Read Genesis 13

What was Abram's financial situation? (v. 1-2)
___

Why did Abram and Lot separate from each other? (v. 3-13)
___

What did God promise Abram, and what did Abram do? (v. 14-18)
___

Day 4: Read Genesis 14

What did Abram do for Lot and why? (v. 1-17)
___

Who was Melchizedek and how did Abram respond to him? (v. 18-20)
___

Why did Abram refuse gifts from the king of Sodom? (v. 21-24)
___

Day 5: Read Genesis 15

What was Abram concerned about? (v. 1-3)
___

What did God promise and what was Abram's response? (v. 4-6)
___

What did Abram ask for and what did God ask him to do? (v. 7-10)
___

Describe what you understand of this prophecy. (v. 11-21)
___

For Further Study

Key Verse: "And he believed in the Lord, and He accounted it to him for righteousness."

Genesis 15:6

Lesson 4

Overview

These chapters have some very difficult situations to process. One outstanding thought for every believer should be that even when we make mistakes, God is still gracious and still in control of everything.

Keep in mind that Abram and Sarai were their original names, but God renamed both of them to the more familiar Abraham and Sarah. Both sets of names had meanings, which were very important to the people of that day. Names had to do with character and purpose, and in some cases even reputation.

Spend some time with the more difficult chapters trying to imagine how the people of that day dealt with their culture. Some issues, like marrying more than one wife, were common among pagan cultures, but that practice was definitely not God's will. It was very easy even for people of God to get mixed up with ungodly ideas and turn from God's will for their lives. It was a big temptation for them, and it still is a big temptation today. That is one of the compelling reasons to read God's Word carefully and thoughtfully. If we stay close to God's Word, we will be less inclined to get caught up in the culture of our day that draws our hearts and lives away from God. We read in this lesson how both Abraham and Lot got caught up in ungodliness, and we see the disastrous consequences.

Several times during the life of Abraham, God confirmed His covenant with Abraham and his descendants. Abraham's family became the chosen people of God. It would be through Abraham's line that God's Messiah would come. You will see through the entire Old Testament how God protected and provided for the lineage of our Savior.

Lesson 4

Daily Bible Study

Day 1: Read Genesis 16

Why did Abram marry Hagar? (v. 1-3)

Why was Sarai upset? (v. 4-5)

What happened to Hagar? (v. 6-9)

How did the Angel of the Lord encourage Hagar? (v. 10-16)

Day 2: Read Genesis 17

How was Abraham's name change tied to God's covenant with him? (v. 1-5)

Name some other parts of the covenant (v. 6-9)

How was circumcision part of the covenant? (v. 10-14)

Why did Abraham laugh? (v. 15-17)

What would become of Ishmael? (v. 18-27)

Day 3: Read Genesis 18

What did Abraham think of his guests? (v. 1-5)

What did Abraham do for them? (v. 6-8)

Why did Sarah laugh and why did she lie about it? (v. 9-15)

_____

What was wrong with Sodom and Gomorrah? (v. 16-21)

What did Abraham ask for and why? (v. 22-33)

_____

Day 4: Read Genesis 19

Why did Lot want the angels to stay with him? (v. 1-5)

_____

What awful thing was Lot willing to do and what was the result? (v. 6-11)

_____

What was the main problem with Lot's family? (v. 12-16)

_____

What happened? (v. 17-29)

_____

Why did Lot's daughters do this terrible deed? (v. 30-38)

_____

Day 5: Read Genesis 20

Why did Abraham lie? (v. 1-2)

_____

How did Abimelech know the truth? (v. 3-7)

_____

How did Abraham justify his lie? (v. 8-13)

_____

What was the result? (v. 14-18)

_____

For Further Study

Key Verse: "Then she called the name of the Lord who spoke to her, You-Are-the-God-Who-Sees; for she said, 'Have I also here seen Him who sees me?' "

Genesis 16:13

Lesson 5

Overview

The story of Abraham is not only the history of the chosen people of God, but it is also full of lessons for our own Christian lives. Abraham and Sarah were incredibly blessed by God, but they were by no means perfect. God in His wisdom recorded the good and the bad so that we might see His grace, mercy and sovereignty.

This is a good time to be sure that your beliefs about these people and events line up with what the Bible says. It is amazing how many people see movies or books that depict someone's ideas about Bible stories, and then have trouble remembering which facts were actually in the Bible. Pay careful attention to your reading so that you do not get someone else's imagination confused with the inspired Word of God.

These chapters tell the remarkable story of the birth of Isaac to Abraham and Sarah in their old age. We see the conflict between Ishmael and Isaac, which still rages on to this day. A great lesson to us is that we must never violate God's will in order to help God accomplish His purpose. We are honored when God uses us to further His kingdom, but we must always follow His will. Abraham and Sarah knew they had a promise from God about a son, but they were too impatient to wait for God's timing. And then when God did send them a son, the conflict between God's ways and man's ways proved too much for them to live with.

Ishmael's descendants and Isaac's descendants have been at war almost ever since this first account. We must remember that the son of God's promise was Isaac, and the land of Israel belongs to Isaac's descendants. We will be studying the land and God's people for many months to come as we read this amazing account of God's covenant with Abraham.

Lesson 5

Daily Bible Study

Day 1: Read Genesis 21

What was Sarah's son's name? (v. 1-3)

___

What did Sarah learn in her laughter? (v. 4-7)

___

Why was Sarah upset and what was the result? (v. 8-13)

___

What happened to Hagar and Ishmael? (v. 14-21)

___

What was Abraham's name for God at Beersheba? (v. 22-34)

___

Day 2: Read Genesis 22

What did God tell Abraham to do, and what was his response? (v. 1-3)

___

How is Abraham's faith shown? (v. 4-8)

___

Considering Abraham's age, how is Isaac's faith shown? (v. 9-10)

___

Why did God say He would bless the nations through Abraham? (v. 11-24)

___

Day 3: Read Genesis 23

Did Abraham and the Canaanites consider the land to belong to Abraham? (v. 1-9)

___

What was the relationship between Abraham and the Canaanites? (v. 1-9, again)

___

Why did Abraham want to pay for the land? (v. 10-16)

Where was Sarah buried? (v. 17-20)

Day 4 – Read Genesis 24

What did Abraham want his servant to do? (v. 1-4)

What was the servant's concern and Abraham's response? (v. 5-9)

What was the servant's prayer and the result? (v. 10-21)

Do you know why the servant was so deeply grateful? (v. 22-27)

After the servant told the whole story, what was the response from Rebekah's brother and father? (v. 28-51)

What did the servant want to do and what was Rebekah's response? (v. 52-61)

How did Isaac feel about Rebekah? (v. 62-67)

Day 5 – Read Genesis 25

Write anything that stands out to you about Abraham's death and burial. (v. 1-18)

What happened with Esau's birthright? (v. 19-34)

For Further Study

Key Verse: "And Abraham called the name of the place, The-Lord-Will-Provide; as it is said to this day, 'In the Mount of the Lord it shall be provided.' "

Genesis 22:14

Lesson 6

Overview

We will take a break from Genesis and spend some time in the book of Job. It will seem like we are skipping over to Job, and in a sense we are. But it's not what it seems. We want this study to be chronological, and historically the events of Job happened sometime during the events of Genesis. The most likely place is around Genesis 10-12.

In the order of the books of the Bible, Job is positioned with the poetry books because most of it is written as a poem. But again, most Bible scholars put the events of Job somewhere in the time of Genesis. The reasons for that include: no nations or rulers are mentioned in the book of Job; the Levitical sacrificial system had not yet been established; the Israelites are not mentioned; and dinosaurs were not yet extinct. Of course the word "dinosaur" is not mentioned since it did not become a word until the 1800s. Job uses "leviathan" and "behemoth" for the dinosaurs.

We will not read the entire book of Job at this time, although it is definitely worth reading every chapter. We will read enough to get the general idea of Job's life and his interaction with his "friends". Many people mistakenly assume that Job is a book to help us understand the purpose of suffering in this life. But if that were the purpose, then the answer is not really given. We see that God granted Satan permission to attack Job in every way. Satan was given permission to attack Job's possessions and kill his children first. Then God lets him attack Job's health. Even Job's wife turned against God and against Job. Then his friends come to "comfort" him. We see Job's friends taking the position that his sufferings are basically his own fault. There are great lessons to learn about how to comfort someone who is having hard times in their life. Next week there will be great lessons about all of life.

Lesson 6

Daily Bible Study

Day 1: Read Job 1

How is Job described? (v. 1-5)

_____
_____

How did Satan describe Job? (v. 6-12)

_____
_____

What happened to Job and why? (v. 13-19)

_____
_____

How did Job respond? (v. 20-22)

_____
_____

Day 2: Read Job 2

How did God describe Job? (v. 1-3)

_____
_____

How did Satan describe him? (v. 4-5)

_____
_____

What happened next and what was Job's response? (v. 6-10)

_____
_____

How long were Job's friends silent and why? (v. 11-13)

_____
_____

Day 3: Read Job 3

What did Job wish for? (v. 1-10)

_____
_____

What was his next thought? (v. 11-19)

_____

_____

What was his final thought in this chapter? (v. 20-26)

_____

_____

_____

Day 4: Read Job 4

How did Eliphaz describe Job? (v. 1-6)

_____

_____

What did Eliphaz say was the cause of Job's suffering? (v. 7-11)

_____

_____

Describe his vision. (v. 12-21) Based on God's description of Job, was Eliphaz correct?

_____

_____

_____

Day 5: Read Job 8

What did Bildad claim was the reason for Job's suffering? (v. 1-4)

_____

_____

What did Bildad accuse Job of? (v. 5-14)

_____

_____

How did Bildad claim Job's joy would return? (v. 15-22)

_____

_____

Considering what God said of Job in chapters 1 and 2, was Bildad right?

_____

_____

For Further Study

Key Verse: "There was a man in the land of Uz, whose name was Job; and that man was blameless and upright, and one who feared God and shunned evil."

Job 1:1

Lesson 7

Overview

This week we will return to the purpose of the book of Job. If the purpose were to understand suffering, all we are really left with is that sometimes God allows suffering for His own reasons. And sometimes we are not able to understand God's reasons. In those cases, He wants us to trust His power and purpose.

Most of the chapters from chapter 4 through chapter 37 are lengthy discourses on Job's situation given by his so-called friends. Throughout those chapters Job's friends offer reasons for his pain. Those chapters are definitely worth reading, but in this study we will read only a few representative chapters. Job's friends blame his suffering on his own sinful life, while Job continues to maintain that he had led a Godly life. The arguments go on and on with each friend contributing his own ideas. Most of the individual discourses last only one or two chapters; then we come to Elihu. Since he admits he was the youngest, he stayed quiet until the others seemed to have finished. Then he gives his views for six chapters! In chapter 38, God gives His opinion of all these words the three friends offered to His servant Job.

Then we see God addressing Job and causing Job to focus on His omnipotence and omniscience (two big words that mean God is all-powerful and all-knowing). God never tells Job why he had to suffer. God never mentions to Job anything about His conversations with Satan. He spends four chapters questioning Job about the universe in general and Job's experiences in particular. Again, He never addresses Job's personal suffering. We know God could have prevented it, but He didn't. The main lesson seems to be to trust God's ways as higher than our own, no matter what happens. In the end, Job learns to trust God's plan for his life, and his blessings return when he prays for his friends.

Lesson 7

Daily Bible Study

Day 1: Read Job 32

Why did Elihu wait to speak and why was he upset? (v. 1-5)

What did Elihu think about the other men? (v. 6-9)

Why did Elihu think he should speak? (v. 10-22)

Day 2: Read Job 38

What did God say about these men? (v. 1-3)

What are God's questions about? (v. 4-18)

Why do you think God questioned Job about light, snow and rain? (v. 19-30)

What other subjects does God mention? (v. 31-41)

Day 3: Read Job 40

What was Job's first response to God? (v. 1-5)

What did God want Job to consider? (v. 6-14)

What do you think a behemoth is? Give some of the characteristics. Illustrate one if you can. (v. 15-24)

_____

_____

Day 4: Read Job 41

Describe Leviathan. Have you ever seen anything like it? (v. 1-11)

_____

_____

How did Leviathan breathe? What does it remind you of? Give some other remarkable characteristics. (v. 12-21)

_____

_____

Why do you think God spent so much time describing Leviathan? (v. 22-34)

_____

Day 5: Read Job 42

How did Job's attitude change? (v. 1-6)

_____

How did Job's friends' attitudes change? (v. 7-9)

_____

_____

When and how did the Lord restore Job's blessings? (v. 10-17)

_____

_____

Extra: Read any other chapters in Job and write what stands out.

_____

_____

_____

_____

_____

_____

For Further Study

Key Verse: "And the Lord restored Job's losses when he prayed for his friends. Indeed the Lord gave Job twice as much as he had before."

Job 42:10

Lesson 8

Overview

This week we will return to our Genesis study. Remember that in Genesis 25 the death of Abraham and Ishmael is recorded, and the story then focuses on Isaac. We know that Isaac is the son of promise to Abraham, and we recognize the on-going conflict with the descendants of Isaac and Ishmael. The descendants of Ishmael make up a large portion of the Arab nations today, and they continue to war with the nation of Israel, Isaac's descendants. The major conflict today is over the land, and we see in our Genesis study that the land does in fact belong to Israel. There is, however, some controversy over that among Bible scholars.

In this week's study, we will read about Isaac and Rebekah, as well as their twin sons, Jacob and Esau. When you read the Biblical account of these lives, you can see the trouble that comes when a person acts on his or her own rather than looking to God. Often we mentally criticize these people for their failure to trust and obey God when we do the exact same thing in our own lives. It seems easier to spot another person's mistakes than to notice our own.

Isaac and Rebekah certainly had their share of family problems. Most of their problems were a result of disobedience and selfishness. Those problems were passed down to their sons, who also had a lot of conflict between them. The conflict between the brothers was in large part the result of their parents each favoring one son over the other. This caused a lot of grief for their family. Both Isaac and Rebekah made mistakes that made their family situation very unhappy. In the end, Jacob and Esau had the opportunity to reconcile their differences in spite of their parents' mistakes. Again, it is important to note that God's plans were not hindered by the mistakes of Abraham, Isaac and Jacob. They became the forefathers of the nation of Israel, known for their faithful lives.

Lesson 8

Daily Bible Study

Day 1: Read Genesis 26

What did God tell Isaac? (v. 1-5)
_____
_____

What did Isaac do wrong and what happened? (v. 6-11)
_____
_____

What happened with the wells, and what can we learn? (v. 12-25)
_____
_____

Why did Abimelech and his friends come to Isaac, and what was the result? (v. 26-33)
_____
_____

How did Isaac and Rebekah feel about Esau's wives? (v. 34-35)
_____

Day 2: Read Genesis 27

What did Isaac want to do? (v. 1-4)
_____

What did Rebekah do? (v. 5-17)
_____

What did Isaac do? (v. 18-29)
_____

Why was Esau so upset, and what was the result? (v. 30-40)
_____
_____

What was Rebekah's new plan and why? (v. 41-46)
_____
_____

Day 3: Read Genesis 28

Where did Isaac send Jacob specifically? (v. 1-5)

_____

What did Esau do? (v. 6-9)

_____

What did God show Jacob? (v. 10-16)

_____
_____

What was Jacob's response? (v. 17-22)

_____
_____

Day 4: Read Genesis 29

Describe Jacob's first relationships in his journey to find a wife. (v. 1-14)

_____
_____

What did Laban do to Jacob? (v. 15-25)

_____

How long did Jacob work to marry Rachel? (v. 26-30)

_____

How do Leah's sons' names show how she felt? (v. 31-35)

_____

Day 5: Read Genesis 30

What went wrong in Jacob's family? (v. 1-24)

_____
_____

What did Jacob want? (v. 25-26)

_____

What did Laban want? (v. 27-31)

_____
_____

What was the result? (v. 32-43)

_____
_____
_____

For Further Study

Key Verse: "And the Lord appeared to him the same night and said, 'I am the God of your father Abraham; do not fear, for I am with you. I will bless you and multiply your descendants for My servant Abraham's sake.' "

Genesis 26:24

_____
_____
_____
_____
_____
_____
_____
_____
_____
_____
_____
_____
_____
_____
_____
_____
_____
_____
_____
_____
_____
_____
_____
_____
_____
_____

Lesson 9

Overview

What an incredible section of scripture we are about to dive into! These passages contain so many famous stories that have so much to teach us. Always keep in mind that "the Word of God is living and powerful, and sharper than any two-edged sword, piercing even to the division of soul and spirit, and of joints and marrow, and is a discerner of the thoughts and intents of the heart." (Hebrews 4:12) No matter how many times we read and study scripture, God always has new and living lessons for us to apply to our thought processes.

We begin this week with Jacob escaping from his father-in-law, who had deceived Jacob into working for him for many, many years. Jacob has made Laban a very wealthy man, and God has blessed Jacob with wealth and many sons. Having many children in those days was a great sign of power and prestige. God instructs Jacob to return to his own land, the land of his father and grandfather. There is trouble with Laban and anticipated trouble with returning to Canaan where Esau still lives. Would Esau take kindly to the brother who had tricked him out of his birthright and deceived their father with the blessing?

Notice an interesting trait that is passed down to each generation in this famous family of faith and blessing. We see time and again how lies and deception, from Abraham's lying to Pharoah in Egypt to Jacob's sons lying to the men of Shechem. We know Isaac and Jacob both dealt in deception as well. The dishonesty in this family causes pain and rips relationships apart every time, but they do not choose to stop. Later God would write in the Law that the sins of the fathers are passed down to the sons as well. That certainly was the case with each of these fathers. We should carefully consider the importance of learning to walk in Truth; the One we follow is Truth. (John 14:6) Do we feel an urgency to walk in Truth because of possible unpleasant consequences or simply because we want to honor God?

Lesson 9

Daily Bible Study

Day 1: Read Genesis 31

What did God instruct Jacob to do and why? (v. 1-3)
___

How did Rachel and Leah feel about their father? (v. 4-16)
___

What is important about these idols? (v. 17-35)
___

How long was Jacob under Laban's authority, and what did he think of him? (v. 36-42)
___

How did the relationship between Jacob and Laban end? (v. 43-55)
___
___

Day 2: Read Genesis 32

Why was Jacob afraid of Esau? (v. 1-7)
___

What did Jacob do? (v. 8-21)
___

Whom did Jacob wrestle with and why is it important? (v. 22-32)
___

Day 3: Read Genesis 33

How would Leah have felt about this arrangement? (v. 1-2)
___

What happened between Jacob and Esau? (v. 3-17)
___

Where did Jacob settle and what did he call it? (v. 18-20)

Day 4: Read Genesis 34

What happened to Dinah? (v. 1-4)

How did the two families feel about this? (v. 5-12)

What did Jacob's sons want Shechem to do and why? (v. 13-17)

What did Shechem do and why? (v. 18-24)

What did Levi and Simeon do? (v. 25-29)

Why was Jacob upset? (v. 30-31)

Day 5: Read Genesis 35

What did God tell Jacob to do and how did he respond? (v. 1-7)

Give several specific promises God made to Jacob. (v. 8-15)

How was Isaac blessed at the end of his life? (v. 16-29)

For Further Study

Key Verse: "I am the God of Bethel, where you anointed the pillar and where you made a vow to Me. Now arise, get out of this land, and return to the land of your family."

Genesis 31:13

Lesson 10

Overview

Many times we are tempted to skip over long lists of names in the Bible, also known as the genealogies. And even skimming them seems like a lot of trouble. But God put every word in the Bible for a reason, so it is always beneficial to try to see what that reason is. As we have already mentioned, one reason is to show that God is personally interested in individuals, not just nations or groups. In Esau's genealogy, there are many notable names. Notice also that very often the mothers are mentioned as well.

Next we come to the exciting story of Joseph, the dreamer. This story spans the rest of the book of Genesis, even though Joseph was not in the Israelite line to the Messiah. That privilege would come to Joseph's brother, Judah, as unlikely as that seems at first. Again, reading carefully and thoughtfully is very helpful in our understanding of God's Word.

There is another story within the story concerning Judah and his daughter-in-law, Tamar. It seems like a very strange story for our culture, but a careful look shows a woman who wanted to be a part of God's chosen people very desperately. And God blessed her actions, even though they seem terrible to us today. She and her sons are mentioned by name in the genealogies of Jesus.

So, dive into the amazing adventures of a man named Joseph. The lessons for us today are almost limitless. Notice particularly why Joseph was continually blessed by God. But notice also that God took His own sweet time in rescuing Joseph every time. In human terms, we might say God could have prevented so many of Joseph's misfortunes, but He did not do that. In His divine plan, He used Joseph's life to show us that His ways truly are higher than ours, and, like Job, we may not always understand why God does what He does. We simply trust.

Lesson 10

Daily Bible Study

Day 1: Read Genesis 36

What is another name for Esau? (v. 1-8)
_____

Name several notable sons of Esau. (v. 9-19)
_____
_____

Why might the sons of Seir be mentioned? (v. 20-30)
_____
_____

Esau was the father of what people-group? (v. 31-43)
_____

Day 2: Read Genesis 37

Why did Joseph's brothers hate him? (v. 1-4)
_____
_____

Briefly describe Joseph's dreams. (v. 5-11)
_____
_____
_____

What happened in Dothan? (v. 12-36)
_____
_____
_____

Day 3: Read Genesis 38

Why did God kill Er and Onan? (v. 1-10)
_____
_____
_____

What happened with Judah and Tamar and what was the result? (v. 11-26)

What were the twins' names? (v. 27-30) See also Matthew 1:3 for more on these sons.

Day 4: Read Genesis 39

Describe Joseph's situation in Potiphar's house. (v. 1-6)

What did Potiphar's wife do? (v. 7-19)

Describe Joseph's situation in prison. (v. 20-23)

Day 5: Read Genesis 40

Whom did Joseph say gives interpretations? (v. 1-8)

What was the interpretation of the butler's dream? (v. 9-15)

What was the interpretation of the baker's dream? (v. 16-19)

What happened? (v. 20-23)

For Further Study

Key Verses: "The Lord was with Joseph, and he was a successful man; and he was in the house of his master the Egyptian. And his master saw that the Lord was with him and that the Lord made all he did to prosper in his hand."

Genesis 39:2-3

Lesson 11

Overview

This lesson begins with the spectacular story of how Joseph was finally released from prison. There is a danger with stories we have heard all of our lives: we tend to mentally skip over them because we are so familiar with them. Try to form the habit of reading carefully, even those parts you are very familiar with. You might not think of some of the Old Testament happenings as spectacular simply because of familiarity. But these are certainly amazing circumstances for Joseph and for the nation of Israel.

Notice that Joseph was in prison for two years after he had asked the butler to remember his story and try to get him freed. Most of us would be very angry at God for allowing so much time to pass while we are in a difficult situation. But, as Joseph's story powerfully reminds us, God's plans unfold exactly as He wills them to, in His own time. Joseph proved his trust in God's plans over and over in his life, even as circumstances seemed to always come against him. He kept a strong faith and a positive attitude even when wrongfully accused and imprisoned.

Chapter 41 signals the end of much of Joseph's sufferings. But there is still something missing for him. He is still separated in every way from his family. This entire lesson tells the heart-melting story of how Joseph was restored to his family. There are so many spiritual lessons for us in this story. As you read, ask God to help you notice the things He wants to teach you. Try to pinpoint lessons such as why Jacob would not allow Reuben to take Benjamin, but he consented to Judah. Ponder whether Joseph was having a hard time forgiving his brothers, or if he was trying to find out if his brothers had changed. Could he trust his brothers not to harm Benjamin the way he himself had been harmed by them? Try to separate what the Bible really says from what you might have seen in a cartoon or book.

Lesson 11

Daily Bible Study

Day 1: Read Genesis 41

Describe the first dream. (v. 1-4)
___

Describe the second dream. (v. 5-7)
___

What was Pharaoh's problem? (v. 8)
___

What was the solution? (v. 9-14)
___

What did Joseph say about interpretation of dreams? (v. 15-16)
___

What was the interpretation? (v. 17-32)
___

What did Joseph advise Pharaoh to do? (v. 33-36)
___

What did Pharaoh do? (v. 37-46)
___

Who were Joseph's sons? (v 47-57)
___

Day 2: Read Genesis 42

Did Joseph and his brothers recognize each other? (v. 1-8)
___

What did Joseph require of them? (v. 9-24)
___

What was Jacob's response? (v. 25-38)

_____
_____

Day 3: Read Genesis 43

Who convinced Jacob to send Benjamin? (v. 1-14)

_____

Why did Joseph cry? (v. 15-30)

_____
_____

What surprised the brothers? (v. 31-34)

_____
_____

Day 4: Read Genesis 44

How did Joseph test them? (v. 1-17)

_____
_____

What was the result of the test? (v. 18-34)

_____
_____

Day 5: Read Genesis 45

What did Joseph say was the reason he was in Egypt? (v. 1-8)

_____

What did Joseph want them to do? (v. 9-15)

_____

What did Pharaoh do? (v. 16-21)

_____

How did Jacob respond? (v. 22-28)

_____
_____

For Further Study

Key verses: "And God sent me before you to preserve a posterity for you in the earth, and to save your lives by a great deliverance. So now it was not you who sent me here, but God; and He has made me a father to Pharaoh, and lord of all his house, and a ruler throughout all the land of Egypt."

Genesis 45:7-8

Lesson 12

Overview

We come now to the end of Genesis, the end of the book of beginnings. The men we have been studying since Genesis 12 are known as the Patriarchs. That means that these men were strong male leaders in their families. It does not mean that the women were less important. In fact, as we have noticed, the women are given very prominent roles throughout the Bible.

The importance of the promises God made to Abraham, Isaac and Jacob cannot be overstated. If you do not understand the relationship that these men each had with God, then you will not understand the significance of most of the Bible. Their family was set apart as the chosen people of God in order to protect and preserve the genealogical line of the Messiah. So God's promises and dealings with the Israelites are critical to His ultimate plan for the entire world. Hopefully, as you are reading thoroughly and carefully, you are understanding the reasons God gave us this particular information.

So, as you read these last chapters of Genesis, notice who went to Egypt, why they went, where they settled and why. So many things in the Bible make more sense when you understand the background of a given situation. Notice Jacob telling Joseph personally about God's promises. We don't have a record of God appearing to Joseph in the same way He appeared to his father, his grandfather, and his great-grandfather. Part of the reason for that is that those particular promises would not be fulfilled in Joseph's line. As we have already mentioned, the Promise would be fulfilled through Judah. Read carefully through the blessings and prophecies about each of Jacob's sons. Later on we will read about the 12 tribes of Israel, and we will see the significance of the double blessing for Joseph through his sons.

Lesson 12

Daily Bible Study

Day 1: Read Genesis 46

Was it God's will for Israel to go to Egypt and how do you know? (v. 1-4)

How many total Israelites went to Egypt? (v. 5-27)

Why did Joseph want their occupation emphasized? (v. 28-34)

Day 2: Read Genesis 47

What did Pharaoh offer to the Israelites? (v. 1-6)

How were the Israelites treated? (v. 7-12)

How did Joseph deal with the famine years? (v. 13-26)

What did Jacob make Joseph promise? (v. 27-31)

Day 3: Read Genesis 48

What did Jacob say about Joseph's sons? (v. 1-6)

What was Jacob doing? (v. 7-14)

Why was Joseph unhappy? (v. 15-18)

_____

Why did Jacob give Ephraim a greater blessing? (v. 19-22)

_____

Day 4: Read Genesis 49

How did Jacob describe Reuben? (v. 1-4)

_____

What was Simeon's and Levi's worst quality? (v. 5-7)

_____

From these prophetic verses, why do you think Jesus is sometimes called the "Lion of Judah"? (v. 8-12)

_____

What is most interesting to you about the prophecies for these 6 sons? (v. 13-21)

_____

How were Joseph and Benjamin blessed by Jacob? (v. 22-28)

_____

Where did Jacob want to be buried? (v. 29-33)

_____

Day 5: Read Genesis 50

Who made the trip back to Canaan? (v. 1-9)

_____

How did the Canaanites respond? (v. 10-14)

_____

What were Joseph's brothers afraid of? (v. 15-21)

_____

What did Joseph say about his bones? (v. 22-26)

_____

For Further Study

Key Verses: "Joseph said to them, 'Do not be afraid, for am I in the place of God? But as for you, you meant evil against me; but God meant it for good, in order to bring it about as it is this day, to save many people alive.' "

Genesis 50:19-20

Lesson 13

Overview

Exodus continues the riveting story of God's dealings with His people, the Israelites. The word "exodus" actually means "going out". So, as we read in Genesis about how God's chosen people came to live in Egypt, we will read in Exodus about how God brought them back to the land He promised them.

Exodus begins with how the Israelites were living in Egypt and what was happening to them after Joseph was gone and largely forgotten by the current Pharaoh. Again, take care not to confuse what the Bible really says with any movie or video about these events. Media presentations always have some components that are from the imagination of the writers and producers, since not every detail is included in the Biblical account. Be sure to consider the facts from the Bible above someone's opinion or imagination.

We are introduced to Moses in the second chapter. Moses is credited with writing the first five books of the Bible, known as the Pentateuch. So Moses' life is very prominent in scripture and deserves very careful study. Try to develop the habit of considering who the people are in these accounts and where they came from. For example, who were the Midianites, and who was their ancestor? These details can add much richness to your personal study as you see God's plan unfold. There are also many applications to our own lives as we consider long-term consequences to our actions and decisions.

This lesson covers a lot of ground, so take the extra two days this week to look back over what you have studied. This can help you to more effectively "hide God's Word in your heart" (Psalm 119:11). As you ponder what you are reading and studying, God will show you how to apply what you are learning to your own life of obedience and service to Him.

Lesson 13

Daily Bible Study

Day 1: Read Exodus 1

What happened to the Israelites in Egypt? (v. 1-7)
___
___

What did the new Pharaoh fear? (v. 8-10)
___

What did the Pharaoh do and what was the result? (v. 11-14)
___
___

What was Pharaoh's second plan and what was the result? (v. 15-22)
___
___

Day 2: Read Exodus 2

Who was this baby and what happened to him? (v. 1-4)
___
___

How did Moses' mother ultimately get to raise him? (v. 5-10)
___

Where did Moses go and why? (v. 11-15)
___

Who was Moses' wife, and what was his first son's name? (v. 16-25)
___
___

Day 3: Read Exodus 3

Why did God instruct Moses to remove his shoes? (v. 1-5)
___

What problem and solution did God present to Moses? (v. 6-9)
___
___

What two arguments did Moses make, and what were God's responses? (v. 10-15)

_____

What did God say would happen? (v. 16-22)

_____

Day 4: Read Exodus 4

What was Moses' next argument and God's response? (v. 1-5)

_____

What were the two additional "proofs"? (v. 6-9)

_____

What were Moses' next two objections and God's responses? (v. 10-17)

_____

What were God's further instructions? (v. 18-23)

_____

Describe the next three events. (v. 24-31)

_____

Day 5: Read Exodus 5

What plan did Moses and Aaron present to Pharaoh, and what was his response? (v. 1-4)

_____

What did Pharaoh do to the Israelites? (v. 5-14)

_____

How did the Israelites and Moses respond? (v. 15-21)

_____

For Further Study

Key Verses: "So the Lord said to him, 'Who has made man's mouth? Or who makes the mute, the deaf, the seeing, or the blind? Have not I, the Lord? Now therefore, go, and I will be with your mouth and teach you what you shall say.' "

Exodus 4:11-12

Lesson 14

Overview

This lesson begins with God reminding Moses of how He will deliver the Israelites from bondage and the covenant He had made. We already see the Israelites resisting God's will because of their own weak faith. We can be sure that the first few generations of Israel in Egypt kept their faith strong by recounting God's providence in bringing them out of the famine in Canaan. Gradually the people forgot God's power, but God was about to remind them of exactly who He is and what He can do.

The weak faith and weak obedience of the Israelites become something of a theme for the rest of their history and even to this present day. God's dealings with them show His many attributes: His patience, His providence, His deep love for them and willingness to forgive their unbelief and disobedience. They have a cycle to their relationship with God that looks like this:

1. God blesses them
2. They disobey God
3. God allows disaster
4. They repent
5. God forgives and blesses them

And then the cycle repeats over and over. But God continues to show His grace and mercy to His people. Reading these accounts and knowing how this all turns out can sometimes cause us to judge the Israelites for their stubbornness; however, we should consider that we do the same thing in our own relationship with God. We often get off God's path for our lives, and then turn back to Him only after something disastrous happens. As we study the Israelites, let us be mindful of our own faith in God's plans for our lives, or whether we resist His will. Notice the people's responses to God's miracles and Pharaoh's hardness of heart.

Lesson 14

Daily Bible Study

Day 1: Read Exodus 6

What did God want Moses to remind the Israelites? (v. 1-5)

What did God promise them? (v. 6-8)

How did the Israelites respond? (v. 9)

What was Moses' argument and God's response? (v. 10-13)

Who was Moses' and Aaron's great-grandfather? (v. 14-20)

Why was the identity of Moses and Aaron emphasized? (v. 21-27)

How did Moses feel? (v. 28-30)

Day 2: Read Exodus 7

How did God describe the exodus? (v. 1-7)

What happened with Aaron's rod? (v. 8-13)

What happened with the river? (v. 14-25)

Day 3: Read Exodus 8

Describe the second plague; notice the magicians. (v. 1-8)

What was the result? (v. 9-15)

What was the third plague, and what about the magicians? (v. 16-19)

What was the fourth plague, and what did Pharaoh offer? (v. 20-25)

What happened? (v. 26-32)

Day 4: Read Exodus 9

What was the difference between the Israelites and the Egyptians? (v. 1-7)

What changed about Pharaoh's heart? (v. 8-12)

Why did God allow Egypt to become strong? (v. 13-16)

What 2 types of people are described? (v. 17-21)

What was the 7th plague and how did Pharaoh respond? (v. 22-35)

Day 5: Read Exodus 10

What was the response of Pharaoh's servants? (v. 1-7)

What was Pharaoh's response to the 8th plague? (v. 8-20)

What happened between Moses and Pharaoh? (v. 21-29)

For Further Study

Key Verses: "I will take you as My people, and I will be your God. Then you shall know that I am the Lord your God who brings you out from under the burdens of the Egyptians. And I will bring you into the land which I swore to give to Abraham, Isaac and Jacob; and I will give it to you as a heritage: I am the Lord."

Exodus 6:7-8

Lesson 15

Overview

We are studying through an extremely rich and exciting time in the history of Israel. In fact, what we are reading now contains much of the basis for the entire Jewish faith. Keep in mind the overarching theme that these are God's people, chosen to be the family of the Messiah, with special plans, provisions and protection from our God and Father.

We have already studied the first nine plagues that God brought on the Egyptians. Hopefully you noticed the hardening of Pharaoh's heart during God's dealings with him. You may have noticed that in the first four plagues, Pharaoh's heart grew hard against God's will, and it specifically says that he hardened his own heart. Then in the fifth plague, the language changes to God hardening Pharaoh's heart. So the question becomes: did Pharaoh have a choice about his heart after God hardened it? And the answer is before us. As is always the case, God offers grace and mercy to heal our sinful hearts. But it is up to us to accept or reject God's offer of salvation. And just as there are physical laws, such as gravity, that govern the physical universe, so there are spiritual principles that control our hearts and minds. If we, like Pharaoh, continue to reject God, then there will come a day when we will not be able to soften our own hearts towards God. We see many examples of this type of stubbornness throughout the Bible.

So we come to the tenth plague, the death of the firstborn. Notice the Passover blood was applied to the sides and top of the doors, a foreshadowing of the cross of Christ. We also have the miraculous crossing of the Red Sea in this lesson, as well as the pillar of fire and the pillar of cloud. Notice also the number of Israelites that left Egypt and the continuing evidences of their weak faith. Pray for strong faith in your own life as you study.

Lesson 15

Daily Bible Study

Day 1: Read Exodus 11

How did the Egyptians feel about Moses? (v. 1-3)

What was the tenth plague and how did it affect the Israelites? (v. 4-6)

What was Pharaoh's response? (v. 7-10)

Day 2: Read Exodus 12

What were God's instructions, and where was the blood of the lamb to be applied? (v. 1-10)

What is this feast called and why? (v. 11-20)

What did the Israelites do and what did Pharaoh do? (v. 21-30)

Give several interesting facts about the exodus. (v. 31-42)

What were God's instructions for future Passover feasts? (v. 43-51)

Day 3: Read Exodus 13

How would God's Word be remembered? (v. 1-10)

_____

_____

What were they to do with their first-born sons and animals? (v. 11-16)

_____

How did God lead His people? (v. 17-22)

_____

_____

Day 4: Read Exodus 14

Why did God harden Pharaoh's heart? (v. 1-4)

_____

What did Pharaoh do and why? (v. 5-10)

_____

How did the Israelites respond, and how did God protect them? (v. 11-20)

_____

What happened? (v. 21-31)

_____

_____

Day 5: Read Exodus 15

What did Moses and the people sing about? (v. 1-5)

_____

How did they express their deliverance? (v. 6-10)

_____

What are some of the things they sang about God and how people should respond to God? (v. 11-19)

_____

Who was Miriam and what did she do? (v. 20-21)

_____

Describe the water situation. (v. 22-27)

_____

_____

_____

For Further Study

Key Verses: "And Moses said to the people, 'Do not be afraid. Stand still, and see the salvation of the Lord, which He will accomplish for you today. For the Egyptians whom you see today, you shall see again no more forever. The Lord will fight for you, and you shall hold your peace.' "

                                              Exodus 14:13-14

_____
_____
_____
_____
_____
_____
_____
_____
_____
_____
_____
_____
_____
_____
_____
_____
_____
_____
_____
_____
_____
_____
_____
_____

Lesson 16

Overview

The sounds of Israel's songs of praise for the Red Sea miracle were still echoing when the people began to complain against Moses and against God. It can be very frustrating, especially since we know the whole story, to see how quickly these chosen people of God turn away from God's plans for them. We will see this happen over and over throughout the study of the Old Testament, and indeed the entire Bible. Before we judge them too harshly though, we need to examine our own lives and see if we do exactly the same thing. We are all prone to whine when things don't go exactly as we hope or when God's plans don't happen on our own time schedule. We should all consider how much we trust Him, even as we read and study about the Israelites' difficulties in that area.

So the Lord provided manna for the people to eat. It was His daily provision for them, miraculously appearing every day except on the Sabbath. An explanation of that is given in chapter 16. They even eventually complained about the manna. Reading about the manna should remind us of how God provides daily for us. Often we complain that we don't have what we want. In Psalms God calls this "asking for the food of their fancy." (Psalm 78:18) God help us to be thankful for what we have been given.

We come to the giving of the Ten Commandments in this lesson as well. This is perhaps the most well-known event in the Old Testament. It would be difficult to find someone who hasn't at least heard of the Ten Commandments, even if he or she can't name them. Study them carefully this week. It is very easy to imagine that if I go to church every Sunday and act like a good citizen that I am basically obeying all of the commandments. But those two things may not even accomplish the very first commandment. Use this week's study to examine your own heart.

Lesson 16

Daily Bible Study

Day 1: Read Exodus 16

What was their complaint and God's response? (v. 1-5)
___

How did God provide, and what were His instructions? (v.6-19)
___

Why did some of the leftovers spoil and some did not? (v. 20-26)
___

What did they call the food, and how long did they eat it? (v. 27-36)
___

Day 2: Read Exodus 17

What was their complaint and God's response? (v. 1-7)
___

How did the Israelites defeat the Amalekites? (v. 8-13)
___

What did God instruct Moses to do? (v. 14-16)
___

Day 3: Read Exodus 18

What was Moses' relationship with Jethro, and why did Jethro come to see him? (v. 1-7)
___

What was Jethro's response to God? (v. 8-12)
___

What did Jethro see as a problem, and what was his solution? (v. 13-22)

What did Moses do? (v. 23-27)

Day 4: Read Exodus 19

What did God tell them that their part of the covenant would be? (v. 1-6)

What specific instructions did God give them? (v. 7-15)

How did God appear? (v. 16-20)

What further instructions were given? (v. 21-25)

Day 5: Read Exodus 20

Summarize the 1st through 4th commandments. (v. 1-11)

Summarize the 5th through 10th commandments. (v. 12-17)

What were the instructions for the altar? (v. 18-26)

For Further Study

Key Verse: "Now therefore, if you will indeed obey My voice and keep My covenant, then you shall be a special treasure to Me above all people; for all the earth is Mine."

Exodus 19:5

Lesson 17

Overview

The next two lessons in Exodus are God's extremely detailed instructions and further laws for His people. Keep in mind that the Israelites were just coming from 400 years in Egypt, and many of those years were spent in slavery. They had no idea how to govern themselves or how to follow God apart from Egyptian laws and slavery status. God started with the basis of the law in the Ten Commandments; then He spelled out an amazing amount of detail that they would also be responsible for keeping. It is very important to keep in mind that these specific laws were for the Israelites at that time. They were intended to keep order among the 2 million or so people; they were also intended to protect them and to set them apart from other nations and people groups.

Sometimes people who want to discredit God's word will take passages like these on slavery and claim that the Bible condones slavery. In ancient times, before credit cards and bankruptcy courts, if someone had debts they could not pay, they would be forced to sell themselves to their creditors to work off their debt. This was common practice among many nations during that time. It was not a stamp of approval on slavery; rather, it was a way for a person to pay what he or she owed. Of course, as in the Israelites' situation in Egypt, sometimes a group of people or a nation would be made slaves by a stronger nation that had conquered them. This was another result of the sinfulness of the world, not an example of God giving His approval to slavery. Since it was their practice and heritage in Egypt, God gave them specific laws governing how slaves should be treated.

We also begin looking at the intricate details concerning the Tabernacle, as well as the feast days for Israel. Take some time to consider the many details of obedience God required. Does He give us details of obedience as well?

Lesson 17

Daily Bible Study

Day 1: Read Exodus 21

What did the piercing of the ear mean? (v. 1-6)
_____

How were female slaves protected? (v. 7-11)
_____

Name several offenses where the punishment was death. (v. 12-22)
_____

Describe this type of retribution. (v. 23-27)
_____
_____

Describe the responsibilities of animal owners. (v. 28-36)
_____
_____

Day 2: Read Exodus 22

Describe the laws about theft and property. (v. 1-15)
_____

What are some other offenses where death is the penalty. (v. 16-24)
_____

Describe the lending laws and the offerings. (v. 25-31)
_____
_____

Day 3: Read Exodus 23

Name several laws that are applicable to today. (v. 1-9)
_____
_____

Describe the law of Sabbaths. (v. 10-13)
_____

What were the three feasts? (v. 14-19)

Describe the Angel of God. (v. 20-23)

What specific commands did God give about the Promised Land? (v. 24-33)

Day 4: Read Exodus 24

How did the people respond to the covenant? (v. 1-8)

Describe the vision of the glory of God. (v. 9-18)

Day 5: Read Exodus 25

Where did these offerings come from? (v. 1-9)

Describe the ark of the covenant. (v. 10-16)

Describe the mercy seat. (v. 17-22)

Describe the table and its purpose. (v. 23-30)

Describe the lampstand and the lamps. (v. 31-40)

For Further Study

Key Verse: "The sight of the glory of the Lord was like a consuming fire on the top of the mountain in the eyes of the children of Israel."

Exodus 24:17

Lesson 18

Overview

We often see movie versions of Bible times in which everything seems mostly tan with shades of brown mixed in. Of course we recognize that only royalty in those days could afford the much more expensive and rare dyed cloth for their clothes and home furnishings. So, if you are reading carefully and not skimming over these intricate details of the tabernacle, then you might wonder where these Israelite slaves acquired all the beautiful fabric, gold, silver, precious stones, etc. Perhaps you remember in lesson 15 that God told the Israelites to take everything the wealthy Egyptians would give them. And the Egyptians were so beaten down with the plagues that they gave the Israelites everything they asked for. So the Israelites left their slavery in Egypt with much wealth. God was now instructing them to use these valuables to construct the tabernacle of meeting.

If you have studied the New Testament at all, you might recognize a lot of the imagery of our Christian lives is represented in the parts of Old Testament worship. For example, the lampstand that was always to be kept burning represents Christ as the Light of the world in John 8:12. The altar of incense should remind us that we are to be the "fragrance of Christ" to God, to the church and to a lost and dying world (2 Corinthians 2:15). Try to picture each detail of the tabernacle and why God would instruct them in such a detailed way. It is also useful to remember that our very lives are now the temple of God, God's place of meeting with us (1 Corinthians 6:19).

So we see that the details of the tabernacle are not meant to show us how God wants us to build our churches, but rather how he wants us to pay attention to the details of our lives before Him. Keep your own life and worship in your heart and mind as you study the details of this section. Notice also how all of it can represent Christ and His atonement for us.

Lesson 18

Daily Bible Study

Day 1: Read Exodus 26

Give some interesting details about the curtains. (v. 1-14)
_____
_____

Describe the wood frame. (v. 15-30)
_____
_____

Describe the holy place and the Most Holy. (v. 31-37)
_____
_____

Day 2: Read Exodus 27

How would they carry the altar? (v. 1-8)
_____

How big would the court be? (v. 9-19)
_____

Who would attend the lampstand? (v. 20-21)
_____

Day 3: Read Exodus 28

What kinds of garments would Aaron and his sons wear? (v. 1-4)
_____
_____

Describe the ephod. (v. 5-14)
_____
_____

What was remarkable about the breastplate? (v. 15-30)
_____
_____

What message would be worn on Aaron's head? (v. 31-37)
_____

What 2 things would their clothes represent? (v. 38-43)

Day 4: Read Exodus 29

How would Aaron and his sons be set apart? (v. 1-9)

What made up the sin offering? (v. 10-14)

How would Aaron and his sons' clothes be made holy? (v. 15-21)

What were the wave offering and the heave offering? (v. 22-28)

How long would it take to sanctify the altar? (v. 29-37)

What were the daily offerings and their purpose? (v. 38-46)

Day 5: Read Exodus 30

Describe the altar of incense. (v. 1-10)

What was the purpose of the ransom money? (v. 11-16)

What was important about the bronze laver? (v. 17-21)

Describe the anointing oil and the penalty for misusing it. (v. 22-33)

Describe the incense. (v. 34-38)

For Further Study

Key Verses: "I will dwell among the children of Israel and will be their God. And they shall know that I am the Lord their God, who brought them up out of the land of Egypt, that I may dwell among them. I am the Lord their God."

Exodus 29:45-46

Lesson 19

Overview

This is another one of those action-packed lessons that reminds us of both God's sovereignty and man's sinful state before a just and holy God. It begins with Moses still on the mountain of God, receiving the detailed instructions for His people. Bezalel and Aholiab are notable men in several places of this lesson.

We are faced this week with the tragic failure of Aaron and the Israelites in the golden calf incident. Again, we can be so quick to judge their shallow and short-sighted faith, but we must examine our own lives. The roots of idolatry run deep in the heart of man. And as we look into the story of the Israelites' idolatry, we should be repenting of our own tendency to put other gods before God in our hearts. Ask Him to show you as you read and study exactly where your idols are. Perhaps we did not build a golden calf, but we might have put our televisions and computers before God. We make excuses in our hearts about what we watch and what we allow into our minds from the idols of our culture.

Take note of the punishment for breaking the Sabbath law. Spend some time in prayer this week about how casually we observe Sabbath rest in our culture. Often there is no distinction between the world and the church on any given day. Of course we know that the Sabbath (seventh day) is actually Saturday, and that the early church celebrated the risen Savior on the first day of each week (Sunday). But whether we regard Saturday or Sunday as a day of rest and worship, surely we should consider how God would have us regard a holy (set apart) day to honor Him.

Notice also the emphasis that is given to the "gifted artisans". This should cause us to realize that no matter how God has gifted us in our abilities, we can dedicate those gifts and abilities to His service for a blessing to the body of Christ.

Lesson 19

Daily Bible Study

Day 1: Read Exodus 31

Who were Bezalel and Aholiab, and what were they to do? (v. 1-11)

Describe the importance of the Sabbath. (v. 12-17)

Who wrote the "tablets of testimony"? (v. 18)

Day 2: Read Exodus 32

Why were the people unhappy? (v. 1)

What did Aaron do? (v. 2-6)

What was God's response? (v. 7-10)

What was Moses' response? (v. 11-18)

What was Aaron's response? (v. 19-24)

What did the sons of Levi do? (v. 25-28)

How did Moses show his devotion to his people, and how did God respond? (v. 29-35)

Day 3: Read Exodus 33

Why did the people mourn? (v. 1-6)
___

What was Moses' tent called, and why was it important? (v. 7-11)
___
___

What happened between Moses and God? (v. 12-23)
___
___

Day 4: Read Exodus 34

What did God do for Moses and what was Moses' response? (v. 1-9)
___

What was God's warning? (v. 10-16)
___

What other specific commands did God give? (v. 17-28)
___
___

Why did Moses wear a veil over his face? (v. 29-35)
___
___

Day 5: Read Exodus 35

Which commandment was given first priority? (v. 1-3)
___

What were they commanded to bring? (v. 4-9)
___

What were the "gifted artisans" to do? (v. 10-19)
___

Describe their offerings. (v. 20-29)
___
___

Describe Bezalel's and Aholiab's abilities. (v. 30-35)
___
___

For Further Study

Key Verses: "And the Lord passed before him and proclaimed, 'The Lord, the Lord God, merciful and gracious, longsuffering and abounding in goodness and truth, keeping mercy for thousands, forgiving iniquity and transgressions and sin, by no means clearing the guilty, visiting the iniquity of the fathers upon the children and the children's children to the third and fourth generation.' "

Exodus 34:6-7

Lesson 20

Overview

As you begin reading these next chapters, you might feel like you have read this all before; and you would be correct. In previous chapters God has given Moses exact directions for every detail of the tabernacle. Now in these chapters, every detail will be repeated as it is carried out by Moses and the builders and craftsmen. There may be several reasons that God wanted to repeat these details in His Word. Ask Him as you read to show you what He would have you learn from these specific instructions. Sometimes God puts things in the Bible so that we will consider our own lives before Him; sometimes information is given so that we learn more about the nature and character of God. In these chapters there is some of both.

First we might consider how specifically God wanted His people to obey Him. He even told them the colors He wanted the curtains to be. Each facet of the tabernacle was directed by God. As we have mentioned before, this is not particularly a pattern for our own places of worship. The tabernacle was for a specific people in a specific time. It would be replaced later by the temple that would be built by King Solomon hundreds of years later. And then in the New Testament, the temple of God is our own bodies. So one comparison for our worship today may be how many specific details God gave us for our obedience to Him and how casually we treat those admonitions. For example, we are told to be kind and tenderhearted to each other (Ephesians 4:32), and yet we think of all manner of excuses when we want to treat each other unkindly. We are told to love one another (1 John 4:7-8), and we are even given a specific description of love (1 Corinthians 13:4-7). How often are we completely obedient to that message? We are given many explicit commands that we treat very casually. These Exodus passages should remind us to obey God in every detail.

Lesson 20

Daily Bible Study

Day 1: Read Exodus 36

What is remarkable about the offering? (v. 1-7)

If a cubit is about 18 inches, how big were these curtains? (v. 8-18)

Why do you think these intricate details are repeated as they are carried out? (v. 19-38)

Day 2: Read Exodus 37

What was overlaid on the ark? (v. 1-9)

What were the table and all the utensils overlaid with? (v. 10-16)

What were the lampstand and lamps made of? (v. 17-24)

What overlaid the altar of incense? (v. 25-29)

Read 1 Peter 1:13-21, and explain the significance of gold.

Day 3: Read Exodus 38

Why were rings and poles in all of these pieces? (v. 1-7)

What were the outside pieces made of? (v. 8-20)

If you have a table of weights and measures in your Bible, use it to give an estimate of the cost of the tabernacle. If you do not have a chart in your Bible, find an internet source to figure the approximate value. (v. 21-31)

Day 4: Read Exodus 39

What are the prominent colors of the priestly garments? (v. 1-7)

How heavy would the breastplate likely be? (v. 8-21)

Give another reason that each detail is mentioned so many times. (v. 32-43)

Day 5: Read Exodus 40

What specific additional instruction is given? (v. 1-11)

Give any other specific information about Aaron and his sons. (v. 12-15)

How many times is the phrase "as the Lord had commanded" (or the equivalent in your translation) mentioned? (v. 16-33)

Describe the cloud and the fire. (v. 34-38)

For Further Study

Key Verse: "And Bezalel and Aholiab, and every gifted artisan in whom the Lord has put wisdom and understanding, to know how to do all manner of work for the service of the sanctuary, shall do according to all that the Lord has commanded."

Exodus 36:1

Lesson 21

Overview

Bible scholar J. Vernon McGee said that every Christian should develop an understanding of Leviticus in order to understand Jesus' sacrifice for our sin. So we will try to understand Leviticus in this lesson.

Leviticus is the third book of the Pentateuch, which is the Jewish name for the first five books of the Bible. The New Testament calls these books the Law, and ascribes the authorship to Moses. We have already read in Exodus that the tribe of Levi was set apart to be the priesthood for the Israelites. They would be the ones to do the work of the tabernacle and later the temple, as well as administer the sacrifices before God. So the book of Leviticus describes the duties of the priests as well as the details of worship and sacrifice.

Most people do not take the time to read and study Leviticus. There seems to be little correlation between our acceptance of Christ's sacrifice on the cross and the sacrificial system of the Old Testament. Hebrews has some chapters devoted to the correlation, and a careful study of Leviticus gives us even more insight into our worship of our holy God. But also as in Job, it is very helpful for Bible study and Bible understanding to read all of the chapters. But also, as Job, we will read representative chapters rather than the entire book. Some of Leviticus is very tedious and difficult to study, but it is definitely worth the effort. Try to take notes on the chapters that we don't read in this study.

Keep in mind that the details of the law were specifically for the Israelite people of that day. That is why we do not offer blood sacrifices since Jesus' death on the cross. But also remember that Jesus said he did not come to abolish the law, but to fulfill it (Matthew 5:17). Ask God for particular understanding in Leviticus.

Lesson 21

Daily Bible Study

Day 1: Read Leviticus 10

What key phrase in verse 1 shows the seriousness of this offense? (v. 1-3)

Why did Moses tell them not to show grief? (v. 4-7)

What were the next instructions? (v. 8-13)

How did Aaron defend their actions? (v. 14-20)

Day 2: Read Leviticus 16

What was the difference between the two goats? (v. 1-10)

What did the scapegoat represent, and what was to be done with it? (v. 11-22)

Since God commanded the Day of Atonement to be a yearly sacrifice, what is comparable in our yearly holy days? (v. 23-34)

Day 3: Read Leviticus 17

What is the true blood that makes atonement for our souls (of which the blood of animals is a substitute or symbol)? (v. 1-11)

What repeated phrase shows the significance of the blood? (v. 12-16)

Day 4: Read Leviticus 19

Describe another type of offering. (v. 1-8)
_____
_____

How would the poor be provided for? (v. 9-18)
_____
_____

In this list of further laws, what stands out to you? (v. 19-37)
_____
_____

Day 5: Read Leviticus 23

In the list of prescribed feasts, what has first priority? (v. 1-3)
_____

Describe the first feast to be celebrated. (v. 4-5)
_____
_____

Describe the second feast. (v. 6-8)
_____
_____

Describe the Feast of the Firstfruits. (v. 9-14)
_____
_____

Describe the Feast of Weeks. (v. 15-22)
_____
_____

Describe the Feast of Trumpets. (v. 23-25)
_____
_____

Describe the Day of Atonement. (v. 26-32)
_____
_____

Describe the Feast of Tabernacles. (v. 33-44)
_____
_____

For Further Study

Key Verse: "For the life of the flesh is in the blood, and I have given it to you upon the altar to make atonement for your souls; for it is the blood that makes atonement for the soul."

Leviticus 17:11

Lesson 22

Overview

The book of Numbers is much more than the record book of the Israelites. It is also a chronicle of the forty years of wilderness wandering and a sober account of the blessings of obedience and the consequences of disobedience.

As with Job and Leviticus, we will read only representative chapters in this study. But remember, it is very useful to read and study all of the chapters. Take notes in the same way the study questions are formulated: what does each section actually say?

Numbers begins with a census commanded by God and the results. It continues with more order and organization for the Israelite people. We notice again the special provisions for the Levites and for Aaron and his sons. Chapter 6 gives us the outline of the Nazirite laws, interesting provisions that will show us the background of accounts such as Samson and John the Baptist.

We will actually pick up our study in chapter 9. Numbers has many thought-provoking conversations between Moses and God. It is a good idea to think through what the Bible says about God's omniscience (all-knowing) and His omnipotence (all-powerful). 1 Samuel 2:3 ("For the Lord is the God of knowledge...") and Psalm 62:11 ("power belongs to God.") are good places to start your thinking. It is easy to apply our own limited understanding to individual passages in the Bible and forget the true nature of God revealed throughout all scripture. For example, when God asks Moses questions, is it because God lacks knowledge and needs Moses to inform Him? And when God offers Moses opportunities to take a different path from the one already given, does God wonder what Moses will do? Think on these ideas as you study.

Lesson 22

Daily Bible Study

Day 1: Read Numbers 9

What did God command and what did they do? (v. 1-5)

What was the problem and how was it resolved? (v. 6-14)

Describe the cloud and fire and their purpose. Is there a comparison to God's leading Christians today? (v. 15-23)

Day 2: Read Numbers 11

Why was God displeased and what happened? (v. 1-3)

Why were they complaining? (v. 4-10)

How did Moses respond? (v. 11-15)

How did God respond? (v. 16-23)

What happened? (v. 24-30)

Describe the quail situation. (v. 31-35)

Day 3: Read Numbers 12

What was different about God's communication? (v. 1-4)

What did God say about Moses? (v. 5-8)

What happened and why? (v. 9-16)

_____

_____

Day 4: Read Numbers 13
What were these men supposed to do? (v. 1-16)

_____

What were they specifically to look for? (v. 17-22)

_____

What did they find? (v. 23-29)

_____

What was the argument about? (v. 30-33)

_____

_____

Day 5: Read Numbers 14
How did the people respond? (v. 1-4)

_____

_____

What did Joshua and Caleb say? (v. 5-9)

_____

What did God offer Moses? (v. 10-12)

_____

How did Moses respond? (v. 13-19)

_____

How did God respond? (v. 20-25)

_____

Describe their punishment. (v. 26-38)

_____

What did the people do and why? (v.39-45)

_____

_____

For Further Study

Key Verse: "At the command of the Lord they remained encamped, and at the command of the Lord they journeyed; they kept the charge of the Lord, at the command of the Lord by the hand of Moses."

Numbers 9:23

Lesson 23

Overview

Our second lesson in Numbers will reveal even more truths about God's power and knowledge, as well as emphasizing His holiness. All of these attributes of God are displayed throughout the Bible, and Numbers provides tremendous insight into the nature of the God we serve. Remember it is very helpful to ponder the many passages that describe God so that we may have greater understanding of the way God responds to His people during this critical time in their history.

Chapter 16 presents a startling example of using our own thoughts and ideas instead of God's commands. These men decided that the Levites might not actually be more holy than the rest. They suggested that God was wrong to single out one tribe to lead the people. Even though their argument sounded very spiritual, it was in opposition to God's already stated will. This is a situation that has occurred in religious circles throughout the generations. And it usually has at its core an argument over what God actually said and what men want to reason apart from God's spoken Word. Notice the conflict was not over moral vs. immoral thoughts or actions; rather, it was over a reasonable sounding argument that maybe more people were worthy of leadership than God had commanded. The answer of course was in what God had already commanded instead of human reason.

This kind of situation is exactly why a study like this one can be so helpful to your spiritual growth. You are training your mind to understand what God actually said rather than what a person may have said. Sometimes human words sound really spiritual. So it is extremely important for every child of God to study what God actually said. You may be surprised at times over what you thought the Bible said and what it really says.

Lesson 23

Daily Bible Study

Day 1: Read Numbers 16

What was Korah's complaint? (v. 1-3)
_____
_____

What was Moses' response? (v. 4-11)
_____
_____

Why would Dathan and Abiram not participate? (v. 12-14)
_____
_____

What did Moses want God to do? (v. 15-22)
_____
_____

What did God do? (v. 23-40)
_____
_____

Why were the people upset and what happened? (v. 41-50)
_____
_____

Day 2: Read Numbers 17

According to verse 10, why was the budding of Aaron's rod significant? (v. 1-13)
_____
_____

Day 3: Read Numbers 20

What was Moses' sin and the result? (v. 1-13)
_____
_____

What happened with the Edomites? (v. 14-21)
_____

What stands out to you about Aaron's death? (v. 22-29)

Day 4: Read Numbers 21

Why were the people discouraged? (v. 1-5)

What did God do? (v. 6-9)

Give several names of groups defeated by the Israelites. (v. 10-35)

Day 5: Read Numbers 22

Who was the king of the Moabites? (v. 1-4)

Who was Balaam, and what did Balak want him to do? (v. 5-7)

What did God tell Balaam? (v. 8-13)

Compare Balaam's two responses. (v. 14-21)

What happened with Balaam's donkey? (v. 22-30)

Who did Balak worship? (v. 31-41)

For Further Study

Key Verse: "Then the Lord spoke to Moses and Aaron, 'Because you did not believe Me, to hallow Me in the eyes of the children of Israel, therefore you shall not bring this assembly into the land which I have given them.'"

Numbers 20:12

Lesson 24
Overview

This week's lesson continues the interesting story of Balak, king of Moab, and Balaam, well-known psychic and fortune-teller. Balak was afraid of this mighty group of people called the Israelites, and he wanted to have a curse put on them. He sent for Balaam to do just that, and Balaam heard directly from God. When Balaam's greed began to get the best of him, God sent him a powerful message from a very unlikely source.

This lesson concludes the book of Numbers, but as always, the chapters that are skipped over are certainly not less important. This study is seeking to provide an overview of the Old Testament, but it is very beneficial to read every chapter if possible. If time does not permit, or if you are eager for a general understanding of the entire Old Testament, then commit yourself to going back later and reading the chapters that are not covered in this study. After you have spent time answering questions on each chapter, it should be easy to take notes on chapters on your own. You will have already cultivated the habit of noticing important points and writing them out. Sometimes it can be helpful to simply write down verses that stand out to you as you read.

In some of the skipped chapters, Moses reviews their journey and tells them specifically what the borders for each tribe are. He also explains why two tribes are allowed to settle on the west bank of the Jordan. A review of the journey may have been all new to some in his audience. Remember, God had them wander for forty years so that their parents would all die in the wilderness for their lack of faith, so some of the younger ones may not have heard many of the stories before Moses' review. This new generation would need much greater faith and obedience to accomplish God's will in their new land. Compare their journey of faith with your own.

Lesson 24
Daily Bible Study

Day 1: Read Numbers 23

What did Balak want Balaam to do, and what did Balaam do? (v. 1-12)
_____
_____

What was Balaam's second prophecy? (v. 13-26)
_____
_____

What is Balak determined to do? (v. 27-30)
_____
_____

Day 2: Read Numbers 24

What was Balaam's third prophecy? (v. 1-9)
_____
_____

What were Balak and Balaam's responses? (v. 10-14)
_____
_____

What was the main point of Balaam's fourth prophecy? (v. 15-25)
_____
_____

Day 3: Read Numbers 25

Why was God angry? (v. 1-3)
_____
_____

What was their punishment? (v. 4-5)
_____

Why did Phinehas kill these two? (v. 6-8)
___

What did God say about Phinehas? (v. 9-18)
___

Day 4: Read Numbers 27

What did these women want? (v. 1-4)
___

What did Moses do? (v. 5-11)
___

What did Moses ask for? (v. 12-17)
___

How did God describe Joshua? (v. 18-23)
___

Day 5: Read Numbers 31

Why did they go to war against the Midianites? (v. 1-11)
___

Why was Moses angry? (v. 12-24)
___

What did God tell them to do? (v. 25-31)
___

What was the result? (v. 32-54)
___

For Further Study

Key Verse: "God is not a man, that He should lie, nor a son of man, that He should repent. Has He said, and will He not do? Or has He spoken, and will He not make it good?"

Numbers 23:19

Lesson 25
Overview

This lesson begins the study of the book of Deuteronomy, the last book of Moses. It concludes the section of the Bible known as the Pentateuch, the first 5 books. These books are also known as the law books. At the conclusion of Deuteronomy, we will have a great foundation for the Israelites' entrance into the Promised Land.

The word "Deuteronomy" means literally "the second law" in Greek. The Old Testament was originally written in Hebrew and later translated into Greek and Latin. Deuteronomy is actually more than a retelling of the law; it is Moses' preaching or explaining of the law to this new generation. Like us, they had not witnessed God's mighty hand in Egypt, and possibly many of their faithless parents had not passed down accurate accounts of God's miracles and wonders. Deuteronomy shows us how love and devotion to God from our hearts is far more important than outward religion. But God also shows us that obedience to His Word is the major way we show our love and devotion.

Many people have assumed over the years that the Promised Land is a symbol of heaven. But even though "a land flowing with milk and honey" sounds very heavenly, there is a better comparison for us. In John 10:10 Jesus tells us that He came to give us abundant life. Of course Heaven will be the ultimate abundant life, but the implication is that that the abundant life starts as soon as we trust Him as our Savior. Perhaps it is better to consider the Promised Land as a symbol of our Christian lives now. God was preparing the Israelites to fight in Canaan, to drive out the wicked inhabitants. For that they would need faith in the God who would bring them victory, just as we need for our own Christian journey. We won't have enemies to fight in Heaven.

Lesson 25
Daily Bible Study

Day 1: Read Deuteronomy 1

How many years had passed since they first left Egypt? (v. 1-3)

What two things were they supposed to do? (v. 4-18)

What did the people want before they entered the land? (v. 19-24)

What were they really afraid of, and what was Moses' response? (v. 25-33)

What was God's response? (v. 34-40)

Why were they defeated by the Amorites? (v. 41-46)

Day 2: Read Deuteronomy 2

Why were the Israelites instructed to treat the descendants of Esau respectfully? (v. 1-7)

What had to happen before the Israelites could enter the Promised Land? (v. 8-15)

How would they know whom to fight and whom to respect? (v. 16-25)

Why did God give them King Sihon's land? (v. 26-37)

___

Day 3: Read Deuteronomy 3

How tall was King Og? (v. 1-11)

___

How would they defeat their enemies? (v. 12-22)

___

Why would Joshua and not Moses lead them across the Jordan? (v. 23-29)

___
___

Day 4: Read Deuteronomy 4

How did Moses know his listeners were eager to obey? (v. 1-14)

___

Why is it so important not to carve idols? (v. 15-24)

___

How is God described? (v. 25-31)

___

What is the result of obedience? (v. 32-49)

___
___

Day 5: Read Deuteronomy 5

What was holy and special about these commandments? (v. 1-22)

___

What did God most want from His people? (v. 23-33)

___
___

For Further Study

Key Verse: "Look, the Lord your God has set the land before you; go up and possess it, as the Lord God of your fathers has spoken to you; do not fear or be discouraged."

Deuteronomy 1:21

Lesson 26
Overview

Deuteronomy 6 begins with a famous passage known as the shema', from the Hebrew word meaning "hear". The words are quoted often and by many, as people strive to understand and to live for God. Of course any words can be spoken with no meaning, but these words should penetrate our hearts as a great hymn of praise to our great and awesome God.

Most people don't think of Deuteronomy as a devotional book, but it is a great place to learn about devotion to God. In it, God gives lengthy explanations about how He wants to bless His people and the covenant relationship He desired with them. He emphasizes the obedience that will bring peace and happiness since He knows what is best for His children. Just as loving parents teach a child to obey them for the child's safety, protection and ultimate happiness, so God teaches us to obey Him. He is not forcing His people to simply do His bidding. Rather, He is our loving Father who is always out for our best.

In this lesson, Moses is preaching to the people about what God wants for them. He is reminding them of the sins of their parents and explaining how they came to be the chosen people of God. He tells them of God's promises for the land and for their nation, as well as warning them about what will happen if they do not obey Him. Many people who only casually read the Bible claim that the God of the Old Testament was a God of anger, wrath and judgment. But reading these chapters in Deuteronomy shows us clearly of God's love for His people and His desire to protect them and to have a special covenant relationship with Him. These chapters also serve as a review of all that we have studied and learned about the Israelite nation to this point.

Lesson 26
Daily Bible Study

Day 1: Read Deuteronomy 6

How did God communicate the importance of keeping His Word? (v. 1-9)
___
___

What are some specific rewards of obedience? (v. 10-19)
___
___

Why is learning and understanding history important? (v. 20-25)
___
___

Day 2: Read Deuteronomy 7

What would happen if they did not destroy the enemies of God? (v. 1-4)
___
___

What are some specific reasons God chose Israel? (v. 5-11)
___
___

How were they to overcome their own fear? (v. 12-26)
___
___

Day 3: Read Deuteronomy 8

What are some remarkable facts about their 40 years in the wilderness? (v. 1-4)
___
___
___

When they would become prosperous, what were they to remember to do? (v. 5-10)
_____
_____

What would be the penalty for disobeying God's Word? (v. 11-20)
_____
_____

Day 4: Read Deuteronomy 9

Why was God driving out the Canaanites? (v. 1-6)
_____
_____

How did God describe the Israelites? (v. 7-13)
_____
_____

Why did Moses beg God to save the Israelites? (v. 14-29)
_____
_____

Day 5: Read Deuteronomy 10

What point was Moses making in these verses? (v. 1-11)
_____
_____

Give specific words Moses used to describe and give praise to God. (v. 12-22)
_____
_____
_____
_____

For Further Study

Key Verses: "Hear, O Israel: The Lord our God, the Lord is one! You shall love the Lord your God with all your heart, with all your soul, and with all your strength. And these words which I command you today shall be in your heart."

Deuteronomy 6:4-6

Lesson 27

Overview

Our third lesson in Deuteronomy continues the theme of God's blessings on obedience and curses for disobedience. As we thought about the analogy of loving parents warning their young children of the dangers of disobedience, we understand that God, as our loving heavenly Father wants obedience from us in the same way. He knows that obedience brings not only safety, but also the loving covenant relationship with Him. Just as a disobedient child brings punishment on himself in order to learn, so we as God's children experience the same thing. So rather than think of God as a God of wrath and judgment, let us learn to see Him in the Old Testament as wanting the best for His children.

After chapter 13, we skip quite a number of chapters in order to continue the overview. Once again, these chapters are no less important than the ones we are studying. These particular skipped chapters contain a lot of information about specific laws for the Israelites. We must not take these laws too lightly. Jesus plainly stated that He did not come to abolish the law, but rather He came to fulfill it (Matthew 5:17). But how are we, as Christians, expected to relate to these laws? Should we simply skip over the ones that don't really suit us, for example not eating bacon (Deut. 14:8) or wearing cotton/polyester blend clothes (Lev. 19:19)? And what about tattoos (Lev. 19:28) and haircuts (Lev. 19:27)? Are our views in our culture on these issues displeasing to God? Which of these were cultural/health issues limited to that time, and which were for us to strictly follow today? Why do we embrace some commandments and ignore others? Clearly there are many differing opinions on matters such as these. Different denominations that each claim to interpret the Bible more carefully than others disagree on many of these issues. As you read and study, ask God to help you have understanding.

Lesson 27

Daily Bible Study

Day 1: Read Deuteronomy 11

What is at least one reason Moses would point out these things? (v. 1-7)
_____
_____

What did God promise in return for their obedience? (v. 8-15)
_____
_____

What did God warn them against? (v. 16-21)
_____
_____

What were their two choices and the results of each? (v. 22-32)
_____
_____
_____

Day 2: Read Deuteronomy 12

Give some specific instructions for worship. (v. 1-7)
_____
_____

Where did God want them to worship? (v. 8-14)
_____
_____

Why were they not allowed to eat the blood with the meat? (v. 15-28)
_____
_____

What specific further warning was given? (v. 29-32)
_____
_____

Day 3: Read Deuteronomy 13

What specific sin is worthy of the death penalty here? (v. 1-11)
_____
_____

If a group of people decided to serve other gods, what would the penalty be? (v. 12-18)
_____
_____

Day 4: Read Deuteronomy 26

What would be their testimony and offering at the altar? (v. 1-10)
_____
_____

Why would they be exalted above other nations? (v. 11-19)
_____
_____

Day 5: Read Deuteronomy 28

What is the reason they would be blessed? List some specific blessings. (v. 1-14)
_____
_____

What is the reason they would be cursed? List some specific curses. (v. 15-45)
_____
_____

What would cause God to send a foreign nation to destroy His people? (v. 46-57)
_____
_____

What is God's highest desire for His people? (v. 58-68)
_____
_____
_____

For Further Study

Key Verse: "Today you have proclaimed the Lord to be your God, and that you will walk in His ways and keep His statutes, His commandments, and His judgments, and that you will obey His voice."

Deuteronomy 26:17

Lesson 28

Overview

As Moses is prompting the Israelites to consider their devotion to God, their level of obedience and their journey into the Promised Land, let us use these chapters to consider the same for our own lives. Does God call us to the same level of obedience that He required of His people back then? Are we expected to be obedient to the same things they were? This is the idea that we began in the last lesson. It is definitely worth further study and thought.

Keeping Jesus' words in Matthew 5:17 in mind ("Do not think that I came to destroy the Law or the Prophets. I did not come to destroy but to fulfill."), how should we look at the Old Testament laws? Consider first the reason God did not command the Israelites to be baptized, although baptism is an important component of New Testament faith. Consider also the reason God does not command us to offer sacrifices of animals, yet animal sacrifice was a critical component of Old Testament faith. This is an example of Jesus fulfilling the law. Of course, there must be a sacrifice for sin. Before Jesus came to die, the sacrificial animals were symbols of the Perfect Lamb of God. After Jesus died, we still have a symbol of that sacrifice in believer's baptism. The writer of Hebrews felt compelled by the Holy Spirit to explain all of this in detail. As always, one part of the Bible helps us to understand another part. But the book of Hebrews does not give us details of Jesus' fulfillment of every Old Testament law. Some things we must take by faith and trust the Holy Spirit to teach us (John 16:13). The more we study God's Word, the more we learn and understand how to please Him and deepen our fellowship with Him. Certainly none of us understands everything about how to obey God. We must simply keep trusting Him and looking to His Word for our answers.

Lesson 28

Daily Bible Study

Day 1: Read Deuteronomy 29

What did Moses continually remind them? (v. 1-9)
_____
_____

What did Moses warn should not happen? (v. 10-19)
_____
_____

What would they know if God sent plagues on them? (v. 20-29)
_____
_____

Day 2: Read Deuteronomy 30

How would they be restored to blessing if they disobeyed? (v. 1-10)
_____
_____

What were their choices and their consequences? (v. 11-20)
_____
_____
_____

Day 3: Read Deuteronomy 31

What was Moses' message to Joshua? (v. 1-8)
_____
_____

What were they to do every 7 years and why? (v. 9-13)
_____
_____

What did God predict to Moses and Joshua? (v. 14-30)
_____
_____

Day 4: Read Deuteronomy 32

What was one way they would learn of God's mighty acts? (v. 1-9)
_____
_____

How did they anger God? (v. 10-18)
_____
_____

What would cause God not to completely destroy them? (v. 19-27)
_____
_____

Who would provide their atonement? (v. 28-43)
_____
_____

What did God do for Moses? (v. 44-52)
_____
_____

Day 5: Read Deuteronomy 33-34

Which 4 tribes were blessed first? (33:1-12)
_____
_____

Name the two tribes that came from Joseph. (33:13-17)
_____
_____

What stands out to you in these prophecies? (33:18-29)
_____
_____
_____

How is Moses described? (34:1-12)
_____
_____
_____

For Further Study

Key Verses: "But the word is very near you, in your mouth and in your heart, that you may do it. See, I have set before you today life and good, death and evil, in that I command you today to love the Lord your God, to walk in His ways, and to keep His commandments, that you my live and multiply; and the Lord your God will bless you in the land which you go to possess."

Deuteronomy 30:14-16

Lesson 29

Overview

This lesson begins the exciting and fast-paced book of Joshua. Moses has died, and Joshua is appointed as the new leader for Israel. The book begins with God giving a special message of encouragement to Joshua. Remember that when Moses sent the twelve spies into Canaan, Joshua and Caleb were the only two who had faith that God would do what He had promised. Now forty years have passed, and the entire faithless generation except Joshua and Caleb has died in the wilderness. From the group that left Egypt, only Joshua and Caleb get to enter the Promised Land.

We come to the second spy story for the Israelites as Joshua sends spies to Jericho to see what they need to do to prepare for battle. We read about the faith of a prostitute named Rahab, who is blessed to become one of the ancestors of Jesus. Her name is mentioned in Jesus' lineage in Matthew, along with some other women of faith. It is helpful to note that God was willing to save a Canaanite woman who trusted in Him.

Another water miracle happens in this lesson. We read about the crossing of the Jordan River. You might notice that this crossing is a little different from the Red Sea crossing. For one thing, the Israelites are not running from their enemies; rather, they are triumphantly marching into the land God promised them. Interestingly, the water was stopped only after the priests stepped into it. The memorial stones in the river and on the bank are also interesting to read about.

As you study, notice how often God tells them not to be afraid. Ask God to show you, as you read, what you can learn about your own Christian life. In the same way that He promised to go before them and give them victory in the land, He promises to be with us too (Matthew 28:20, for example). He wants us to trust Him for victories in our lives as well.

Lesson 29

Daily Bible Study

Day 1: Read Joshua 1

What specific command did God give Joshua and why? (v. 1-9)
_____
_____
_____

What was expected of the tribes of Reuben, Gad and the half tribe of Manasseh and why? (v. 10-18)
_____
_____
_____

Day 2: Read Joshua 2

How did the Israelite spies escape the king of Jericho? (v. 1-7)
_____
_____

Describe Rahab's knowledge of God. (v. 8-13)
_____
_____

What did Rahab have to do to be saved? (v. 14-21)
_____
_____

What did the spies report to Joshua? (v. 22-24)
_____
_____

Day 3: Read Joshua 3

What special instructions were given for the ark of the covenant? (v. 1-6)
_____
_____

How did Joshua say they would know that God was with them?

(v. 7-10)
___

What happened at the Jordan River? (v. 11-17)
___
___

Day 4: Read Joshua 4

What was the reason for taking stones out of the Jordan River? (v. 1-8)
___

How did the Israelites feel about Joshua? (v. 9-14)
___
___

Why did God show them these miracles? (v. 15-24)
___
___

Day 5: Read Joshua 5

Why did they need to be circumcised? (v. 1-7)
___
___

What happened to the manna? (v. 8-12)
___

Describe Joshua's meeting. (v. 13-15)
___
___
___
___
___

For Further Study

Key Verse: "This Book of the Law shall not depart from your mouth, but you shall meditate in it day and night, that you may observe to do according to all that is written in it. For then you will make your way prosperous, and then you will have good success."

Joshua 1:8

Lesson 30

Overview

Hopefully as you study through the Old Testament, you are gaining a greater appreciation for what God wants to teach us through this part of His Word. As you carefully read and study these sometimes familiar accounts, look for details you may have missed in previous lessons or sermons. No matter how many times we study a certain passage, God always has a message to deepen our relationship with Him.

We begin this lesson with the exciting and unusual conquest of Jericho. This is the first battle that the Israelites faced in taking over the Promised Land. Keep in mind as you read about the Israelites in Canaan that God was using His people as an instrument of judgment on the idol-worshipping Canaanites. But each individual Canaanite had the opportunity to know God and to turn to Him to be saved. Rahab is a perfect example of this.

Notice that the battle of Jericho was not fought in a usual way. God instructed the Israelites in very specific ways, and their victory would only be guaranteed if they followed God's instructions exactly. He did not want them to put their own logical ideas into His plan. This is a very good lesson for us. Sometimes we know what God wants us to do, but our human logic causes us to disobey. An example of this is when God tells us to love our enemies and to pray for those who are mean to us (Matthew 5:44). But we often fail to do either of these since they go against what we want to do. The Israelite defeat at Ai shows how important complete obedience is to God. In our New Testament grace outlook, sometimes we forget that.

Another important principle is learned in the treaty with the Gibeonites. God specifically tells us what went wrong there, and their actions had long-range negative consequences for them. May we all learn to be completely obedient in every way.

Lesson 30

Daily Bible Study

Day 1: Read Joshua 6

What were God's specific instructions? (v. 1-5)
_____
_____

What did the people do, and what was Joshua's additional instruction? (v. 6-15)
_____
_____

What warning is given? (v. 16-18)
_____
_____

What happened, and who was saved? (v. 19-27)
_____
_____

Day 2: Read Joshua 7

Why was God angry? (v. 1)
_____
_____

What happened at Ai? (v. 2-9)
_____
_____

Describe the consequences and the lessons learned. (v. 10-26)
_____
_____

Day 3: Read Joshua 8

What was different about God's instructions at Ai and at Jericho? (v. 1-2)
_____
_____

What was the battle plan? (v. 3-8)

What were the results of the battle? (v. 9-29)

What did Joshua do, and how long do you think it took? (v. 30-35)

Day 4: Read Joshua 9

What did the Gibeonites do and why? (v. 1-6)

What mistake did the Israelites make? (v. 7-14)

What happened to the Gibeonites? (v. 15-27)

Day 5: Read Joshua 10

What did God promise Joshua? (v. 1-8)

Describe the two miracles. (v. 9-15)

What happened to the 5 kings? (v. 16-27)

How do we know God was pleased with these battles? (v. 28-43)

For Further Study

Key Verse: "Then Joshua said to them, 'Do not be afraid, nor be dismayed; be strong and of good courage, for thus the Lord will do to all your enemies against whom you fight.' "

Joshua 10:25

Lesson 31

Overview

This lesson will conclude the overview of Joshua and begin the study of Judges. Again, the skipped chapters are no less important, and if you have the time to read them and take notes, it is well worth the effort.

Chapter 22 shows us the conflicts that the Israelites would have with each other. This particular conflict is a good example of how to handle situations in which actions for God's glory are misunderstood. Often we find the worst conflicts over different ways of serving God. This conflict shows a diplomatic solution that can be applied to misunderstandings today. The resolution came through both sides communicating with each other and being willing to listen to the other side of the disagreement. It helps to note that they were interested in keeping the other side from sinning against God and bringing punishment on their kinsmen. This is an example of how these Old Testament stories can easily apply to our lives; when faced with a disagreement, be willing to listen to the other person's side. And we have the continual reminder throughout the Old Testament that God required absolute obedience to His Word. He requires our obedience as well. We do not make up our own form of worship and discipleship; we follow what God said.

We have Joshua's farewell address to the Israelites with his famous "Choose you this day whom you will serve" (24:15) challenge. That is still our challenge today.

Next we come to the book of Judges. We will not read all of the chapters of Judges, but again, read them if you can. There are many exciting and famous stories and people in this book. Judges can be a surprising book to study because of its raw details about Israel's disobedience to God. It is sometimes easy to criticize the Israelites' failures, but instead let this study cause us to look deeply into our own level of obedience to God.

Lesson 31

Daily Bible Study

Day 1: Read Joshua 22

Which tribes had land east of the Jordan? (v. 1-9)
_____
_____

Why were the tribes west of the Jordan angry? (v. 10-18)
_____
_____

What was their defense? (v. 19-29)
_____
_____

How did Phinehas and the rest of the Israelites respond? (v. 30-34)
_____
_____

Day 2: Read Joshua 23

What was Joshua's warning about the remaining Canaanites? (v. 1-8)
_____
_____

What important reminders does Joshua give them? (v. 9-16)
_____
_____
_____

Day 3: Read Joshua 24

What high points of Israel's history does Joshua mention? (v. 1-7)
_____
_____
_____
_____

What was Joshua's great declaration of faith? (v. 8-15)

What did the people declare? (v. 16-24)

What memorials did they build? (v. 25-33)

Day 4: Read Judges 1

How were the Israelites demonstrating continued obedience? (v. 1-10)

What details of these conquests stand out to you? (v. 11-26)

What compromises in obedience are highlighted? (v. 27-36)

Day 5: Read Judges 2

What problem had come up? (v. 1-10)

What was God's response? (v. 11-15)

What cycle was begun among the Israelites? (v. 16-23)

For Further Study

Key Verses: "The Lord gave them rest all around, according to all that He had sworn to their fathers. And not a man of all their enemies stood against them; the Lord delivered all their enemies into their hand. Not a word failed of any good thing which the Lord had spoken to the house of Israel. All came to pass."

Joshua 21:44-45

Lesson 32

Overview

Judges shows a clear pattern in Israel's relationship with God. It is something that we should consider carefully in our own relationship to God. We will see this pattern often:

1. Enjoying God's blessings
2. Turning from God's ways
3. Receiving God's judgment
4. Repenting of their sins
5. God's forgiveness and blessings

Then they would repeat the cycle. This happened over and over in the nation of Israel. The Israelites had specific commandments of God that they were to follow. But like us, they often went their own ways instead. This would bring consequences for their wrong actions. When they realized they were under God's judgment for their sins, they would repent, and God would forgive them. He is always willing to forgive our sins.

This lesson has the interesting story of Deborah, the only female judge of Israel. Casual Bible readers may mistakenly think that the Bible somehow puts women lower than men. But careful study shows the opposite. We also read the humorous story of Eglon, apparently a very large man.

We also begin the famous story of Gideon. As you read Gideon's story, try to imagine why the international Bible distributors call their organization the Gideons. Notice that in the beginning Gideon was not eager to take command in Israel. Also, he was not confident of his ability to know whether God was actually calling him or not. But we see God patiently encouraging Gideon towards His will. Look for ways God would speak to your own heart as you read how He spoke to the men and women of the Old Testament.

Lesson 32

Daily Bible Study

Day 1: Read Judges 3

Why did God want them to learn war? (v. 1-6)
___

Why did they become servants again? (v. 7-11)
___

What is an important point in their rescue every time? (v. 12-31)
___

Day 2: Read Judges 4

Who was Deborah? (v. 1-5)
___

What did Barak want? (v. 6-10)
___

What was the result of the battle? (v. 11-16)
___

What happened to Sisera? (v. 17-24)
___

Day 3: Read Judges 5

What is the main message of Deborah's song? (v. 1-9)
___

Which tribes were highly esteemed in this battle? (v. 10-18)
___

How were Jael's actions described? (v. 19-31)

Day 4: Read Judges 6

What did God declare about the Israelites? (v. 1-10)

How did Gideon know who spoke with him? (v. 11-24)

What was Gideon afraid of? (v. 25-27)

Describe the sign of the fleece. (v. 28-40)

Day 5: Read Judges 7

Why did God say Gideon had too many men? (v. 1-2)

How did God reduce the number of fighting men? (v. 3-7)

How did God encourage Gideon? (v. 8-15)

Describe the battle. (v. 16-25)

For Further Study

Key Verses: "Then Deborah and Barak the son of Abinoam sang on that day, saying: 'When leaders lead in Israel, when the people willingly offer themselves, bless the Lord!' "

Judges 5:1-2

Lesson 33

Overview

We finish the account of Gideon in this lesson and begin the story of Samson, perhaps the most famous judge of Israel. Many people do not think of Samson as a judge because he was more known for his strength than his position of authority. His story has many lessons for us. Between Gideon and Samson are several other interesting judges that we will not have time to study. As always, it is a great idea to take some time to read and study them as well.

One important issue in Samson's early life was his disrespect for his parents' views. This caused heartache for his parents and unnecessary trouble in his own life. It is easy for a young person to go his or her own way rather than the narrower road of obedience. Samson's life proves over and over how much better life is when we follow God's will.

Even though Samson was weak in obedience, God still used him. Since Samson judged Israel for twenty years, we know there are many things about his life that the Bible does not mention. Sadly, we remember him most for giving in to Delilah's pleadings and revealing to her the source of his great strength. As we read that particular account, we cannot help but wonder how Samson could have been so foolish. He had quite a temptation towards women, and his failure to resist that temptation was his greatest downfall. We see that he had to give his own life to right the wrongs of his bad decisions.

The rest of the book of Judges chronicles more of Israel's struggles to obey God. They had not obeyed God in getting rid of the Canaanite idols, and they paid a high price for their disobedience. The very last verse of the book of Judges is a sad summary of where they were as a nation. Each person deciding what is right in his or her own eyes is a dangerous place for anyone to live.

Lesson 33

Daily Bible Study

Day 1: Read Judges 8

Describe the conflict between Gideon and Ephraim. (v. 1-3)
_____
_____

What did the leaders of Succoth and Penuel do wrong? (v. 4-9)
_____
_____

What happened with Zebah and Zalmunna? (v. 10-21)
_____
_____

What did Gideon do wrong? (v. 22-27)
_____
_____

What happened after Gideon's death? (v. 28-35)
_____
_____

Day 2: Read Judges 13

How did Manoah's wife know she had spoken with "a Man of God"? (v. 1-6)
_____

What did Manoah want? (v. 7-14)
_____

How did they know the Angel of the Lord? (v. 15-22)
_____

Name two details about Samson. (v. 23-25)
_____
_____

Day 3: Read Judges 14

Why did Samson's parents disapprove of his wife? (v. 1-4)
_____
_____

What happened with the lion? (v. 5-6)
_____
_____

What did Samson's wife do? (v. 7-17)
_____
_____

What happened? (v. 18-20)
_____
_____

Day 4: Read Judges 15

Why did the Philistines kill Samson's wife? (v. 1-6)
_____

Why did the Israelites want to give Samson to their enemies? (v. 7-13)
_____
_____

How did Samson defeat his enemies? (v. 14-20)
_____
_____

Day 5: Read Judges 16

What seems to be Samson's weakness? (v. 1-5)
_____

How did Delilah keep deceiving Samson? (v. 6-14)
_____

Why did Delilah treat Samson so badly? (v. 15-22)
_____
_____

What happened to Samson? (v. 23-31)
_____
_____

For Further Study

Key Verse: "Then Samson called to the Lord, saying, 'O Lord God, remember me, I pray! Strengthen me, I pray, just this once, O God, that I may with one blow take vengeance on the Philistines for my two eyes!' "

Judges 16:28

Lesson 34

Overview

The book of Ruth begins on a sad note but turns into a very happy and encouraging look at God's providence and blessing. There are so many lessons to consider in these four chapters, so spend some time asking God to show you what He would have you learn from this study. Then next time you study Ruth there will be something else for you to consider.

An overarching theme of Ruth is the idea of the "kinsman-redeemer." This was outlined in Moses' law and was strictly adhered to by the Jews, even in these mostly disobedient years of their history. The idea was that, if an Israelite's property was sold or lost in some way, that the closest relative (kinsman) would have the first opportunity to buy it back (redeem it). Naomi and her husband had left their land when they moved to Moab, so their land was presumably sold or simply abandoned. When she moved back with Ruth, who was the widow of her son, she didn't have the money to regain her land. Boaz would act as the kinsman-redeemer of both the land and of Ruth.

The picture of the kinsman-redeemer is another Old Testament picture of what Jesus did for us. He became our Kinsman-Redeemer by purchasing our salvation on the cross. He paid our debt and redeemed us back to Himself with His own blood.

Another interesting part of Ruth's story is how she, as a Moabite, became a part of the line of Christ. She is the third woman mentioned in the genealogy of Jesus in Matthew 1, and none of the three were Jewish. This shows that it was always God's plan to include everyone in His salvation, not just the Jews. The Jews would simply be the instrument God would use to bring Jesus into the world. We will begin the book of 1 Samuel in this lesson, and there is much to learn in this book as well. Samuel's mother Hannah is an inspiring woman as we read about her heartache and how she handled it.

Lesson 34

Daily Bible Study

Day 1: Read Ruth 1

What happened to Naomi's husband and sons? (v. 1-5)
_____
_____

What did Orpah do? (v. 6-15)
_____
_____

What did Ruth do? (v. 16-18)
_____
_____

Why did Naomi want to change her name? (v. 19-22)
_____
_____

Day 2: Read Ruth 2

Who was Boaz? (v. 1-4)
_____
_____

Why did he notice Ruth, and what did he offer her? (v. 5-12)
_____
_____

How did Ruth and Naomi benefit from the situation? (v. 13-18)
_____
_____

What advice did Naomi give to Ruth? (v. 19-23)
_____
_____

Day 3: Read Ruth 3

What further instructions did Naomi give, and what was Ruth's response? (v. 1-7)
_____

How did Boaz respond? (v. 8-11)

What was Boaz's concern, and how did he handle it? (v. 12-18)

Day 4: Read Ruth 4

How did the closer relative respond? (v. 1-8)

How did the elders and people of Bethlehem respond? (v. 9-12)

How were they related to King David? (v. 13-22)

Day 5: Read 1 Samuel 1

Describe the tension in Elkanah's family. (v. 1-7)

What did Hannah vow? (v. 8-11)

How did Eli respond? (v. 12-18)

What did Hannah do? (v. 19-28)

For Further Study

Key Verse: "But Ruth said: 'Entreat me not to leave you, or to turn back from following after you; for wherever you go, I will go; and wherever you lodge, I will lodge; your people shall be my people, and your God my God.' "

Ruth 1:16

Lesson 35

Overview

Hopefully by this time in our study you are seeing the Old Testament as so much more than just a collection of interesting stories. The study of the Old Testament gives us a deeper and richer knowledge of the mighty and merciful God we serve. Without a clear understanding of God's dealings with mankind in the Old Testament, we cannot hope to understand all that Jesus is to us.

In the last lesson we were introduced to Elkanah's family and his wife Hannah in particular. She brought her problem to God, and He blessed her. This week's lesson begins with her prayer of thanksgiving. If you are familiar with the New Testament, you might recognize parts of Hannah's prayer as similar to Mary's prayer in the book of Luke.

Almost immediately we are introduced to the priest Eli's wicked sons. Again, there are many lessons for us as we study through the Old Testament. The fact that Eli's sons "did not know the Lord" (1 Samuel 2:12) should cause each of us to consider whether our own devotion to the Lord has influence on those closest to us. Do they really see God in us?

We also have the amazing story of God's communication with Samuel. Young Samuel was growing up around a strange (but sadly all too common) mixture of Eli's devotion to God and his own sons' corruption. As with each of us, Samuel has a choice to make: hear and obey God or yield to worldly and fleshly temptations. We will see Samuel make a difficult choice to tell Eli the message from God. This is a good time to think about whether you believe the accounts of God's dealings with men and women are absolutely true or not. Did God really call Samuel by name? It is important to know that every word of the Bible is true.

Lesson 35

Daily Bible Study

Day 1: Read 1 Samuel 2

What was Hannah's prayer about? (v. 1-10)

What particular sin did Eli's sons commit? (v. 11-17)

What happened to Hannah? (v. 18-21)

How was Samuel doing? (v. 22-26)

What was the prophecy against Eli's sons? (v. 27-36)

Day 2: Read 1 Samuel 3

What was Eli's instruction to Samuel? (v. 1-9)

Why was Samuel afraid? (v. 10-15)

How did God bless Samuel? (v. 16-21)

Day 3: Read 1 Samuel 4

What happened with the ark? (v. 1-11)

What happened to Eli and his sons? (v. 12-18)

Why did Phinehas' wife name her son Ichabod? (v. 19-22)

Day 4: Read 1 Samuel 5

What happened to the Philistine idol? (v. 1-5)

Why did the Philistines want to send the ark back to Israel? (v.6-12)

Day 5: Read 1 Samuel 6

How would they know that God had struck them? (v. 1-9)

Why did God strike the men of Beth Shemesh? (v. 10-21)

For Further Study

Key Verses: "No one is holy like the Lord, for there is none besides You, nor is there any rock like our God."

1 Samuel 2:2

"And the child Samuel grew in stature, and in favor both with the Lord and men."

1 Samuel 2:26

Lesson 36

Overview

As we study further into the book of 1 Samuel, we get a picture of how the Israelites kept only a partial devotion to God. The idols, false gods and humanist governments of the pagan nations of Canaan had a strong influence on them. Remember that God had instructed them to get rid of all of the pagan people in Canaan, but they had not completely obeyed. The lesson for us should be that if we fail to obey God completely, then there will be negative consequences in our lives. God as our loving heavenly Father knows exactly what is best for us, and He desires that for us. But in His sovereignty He gives us choices. It is up to us to decide our own level of obedience and accept the consequences for our choices.

God continually showed the Israelites how their obedience was directly related to the blessings He would show them. As we read, we wonder how they could have possibly missed that so often. But we must remember that the same thing happens in our own lives. We disobey, have negative consequences, and still wonder how we missed God's blessings. God is eager to bless us as He blessed His people in the Old Testament. But they, like us, often turned to their own ways rather than God's. We notice that sometimes they didn't even know what God required of them because they left off the reading and study of His Word. They even had priests, like Eli's sons and sadly Samuel's sons, who profaned God's Word to the people.

So in this lesson we read about the Israelites' demand for a king. This made Samuel both angry and sad. God had already given instructions for kings in the law, but the people refused to wait for God's timing on that. As always, they suffered in many ways for their insistence on their own will rather than God's. As you study this account, consider how often we refuse to wait for God's timing or decide to do things our own way rather than God's way.

Lesson 36

Daily Bible Study

Day 1: Read 1 Samuel 7

What was the attitude of the people? (v. 1-6)

How exactly were the Philistines defeated? (v. 7-11)

Describe Samuel's relationship with God. (v. 12-17)

Day 2: Read 1 Samuel 8

Why were the Israelites unhappy about Samuel's sons? (v. 1-5)

What was God's response to their request? (v. 6-9)

How did Samuel describe their lives under a king? (v. 10-17)

Why did the people want a king? (v. 18-22)

Day 3: Read 1 Samuel 9

How tall was Saul? (v. 1-2)

Why did the servant urge Saul to go to the "man of God"? (v. 3-10)

How had God prepared Samuel to meet Saul? (v. 11-17)

How did Samuel interact with Saul? (v. 18-27)

Day 4: Read 1 Samuel 10

What would be the two signs that God's Spirit was on Saul? (v. 1-9)

Why did Saul not tell his uncle everything Samuel had said? (v. 10-16)

How did Samuel present Saul as king? (v. 17-27)

Day 5: Read 1 Samuel 11

How did Saul feel about the threat from the Ammonites? (v. 1-6)

What was the result of the battle? (v. 7-11)

How did the Israelites feel towards Saul? (v. 12-15)

For Further Study

Key Verse: "Then Samuel spoke to all the house of Israel, saying, 'If you return to the Lord with all your hearts, then put away the foreign gods and the Ashtoreths from among you, and prepare your hearts for the Lord, and serve Him only; and He will deliver you from the hand of the Philistines.' "

1 Samuel 7:3

Lesson 37

Overview

Chapter 12 is Samuel's speech to the Israelites as Saul is crowned king. Samuel reminds the people that their demand for a king in their own timing showed that they did not trust God. But he also tells them that God still wants to bless them and forgive them for their unfaithfulness. Several lessons are evident for us in this account. First we see that it is indeed profitable for us to understand history. For Israel and for us it is good to be reminded of how God had protected them and provided for them. It is often easier to see God's hand of blessing, protection and even judgment in someone else's life than it is to see Him working in our own life. Israel was about to learn the hard way that it is better to wait for God's timing rather than demand our own. But Samuel also tells them that if they will keep His commandments God will still bless them, even though they had sinned. What a great reminder to us that even in our bad choices, God is still willing to forgive us and restore us to complete fellowship with Him.

Next we see how soon Saul began to do what he wanted to do rather than obeying God. Chapter 13 gives the account of Saul's first act of disobedience. Saul tried to defend his actions, but Samuel told him that God was rejecting him as king after only 2 years. Of course we will see that Saul remained king for 38 more years, during which time God was preparing David to become king. This reminds us that God's timing is often not our timing, and we must be patient to wait on Him. We are introduced to Saul's son, Jonathan, in this lesson, and we see Saul's continued refusal to submit to God's will and the disastrous results. We conclude this lesson with the great story of how David was revealed as king, and how God's thoughts are not our thoughts. Samuel and even David's own father learned that only God knows the heart, while we are quick to judge others based on outward appearances.

Lesson 37

Daily Bible Study

Day 1: Read 1 Samuel 12

Why did Samuel review Israel's history? (v. 1-11)

Why was it wrong for them to demand a king? (v. 12-19)

What hope did Samuel offer to the Israelites? (v. 20-25)

Day 2: Read 1 Samuel 13

What was Saul supposed to wait for? (v. 1-8)

What was Saul's sin? (v. 9-15)

Why did the Israelites have no weapons? (v. 16-23)

Day 3: Read 1 Samuel 14

What did Jonathan want to do and why? (v. 1-6)

What were two results of the battle? (v. 7-23)

What did Jonathan criticize Saul for? (v. 24-30)

How was Jonathan saved from Saul's oath? (v. 31-46)

_____

_____

Who was Abner? (v. 47-52)

_____

_____

Day 4: Read 1 Samuel 15

What did Samuel tell Saul to do? (v. 1-3)

_____

_____

What did Saul do? (v. 4-9)

_____

_____

What lie did he tell Samuel? (v. 10-21)

_____

_____

Why did Saul want to worship God at this point? (v. 22-30)

_____

_____

How did Samuel feel towards Saul? (v. 31-35)

_____

_____

Day 5: Read 1 Samuel 16

How does God choose men for His service? (v. 1-7)

_____

_____

How did Samuel know to anoint David? (v. 8-13)

_____

_____

What did David do for Saul? (v. 14-23)

_____

_____

_____

_____

For Further Study

Key Verse: "So Samuel said, 'Has the Lord as great delight in burnt offerings and sacrifices, as in obeying the voice of the Lord? Behold, to obey is better than sacrifice, and to heed than the fat of rams.' "

1 Samuel 15:22

Lesson 38

Overview

This week's lesson begins with the famous story of David and Goliath. Almost everyone is at least familiar with this story. Was there really a giant, and did young David really kill him with a slingshot? It is important to consider whether you really believe what the Bible has to say.

David's bravery came from his absolute trust in God. Saul's weakness shows what going our own way does to us. Do you remember how tall Saul was? Even if his physical stature should have made him at least a match for Goliath, he had no courage when he needed it most. His faith in himself had brought him to a low point, and his jealousy of David brought him even lower.

This lesson also highlights the blessings of a true and quite unlikely friendship. The relationship between David and Jonathan is remarkable on so many levels. Both young men were drawn to each other as brothers; they had a common love for Saul and a devotion to God. Jonathan would have been next in line for the throne if God had not anointed David. Saul's disobedience to God not only cost him personally, but altered the life of his son as well. We see no jealousy or resentment in Jonathan; rather, we see his loyalty to his friend even though David would take Jonathan's place in the kingdom. Each of us must be careful how we apply this story to our own lives. The lesson here is not to ignore parents' wise counsel in friendships. The account is clear that the effects of sin and rebellion had destroyed Saul's ability to think clearly by this time, and Saul was repeatedly attempting to kill David. Jonathan was protecting both David and his father in his actions.

We should also note that David continued to be loyal to Saul even when Saul was trying to kill him. David trusted God's timing.

Lesson 38

Daily Bible Study

Day 1: Read 1 Samuel 17

Why were Saul and all of Israel afraid? (v. 1-11)
_____
_____

How did David respond to the threat? (v. 12-26)
_____
_____

What did David offer to Saul? (v. 27-32)
_____
_____

How did David say he would beat Goliath? (v. 33-37)
_____
_____

What did David say to Goliath? (v. 38-47)
_____
_____

What were the results of David's actions? (v. 48-58)
_____
_____

Day 2: Read 1 Samuel 18

Describe David's friendship with Jonathan. (v. 1-5)
_____
_____

Describe the relationship between Saul and David. (v. 6-16)
_____
_____

What did Saul hope would happen to David? (v. 17-27)
_____
_____

What happened instead? (v. 28-30)

Day 3: Read 1 Samuel 19

How did Jonathan try to reconcile Saul to David? (v. 1-7)

What went wrong? (v. 8-17)

What happened in Ramah? (v. 18-24)

Day 4: Read 1 Samuel 20

What was David afraid of? (v. 1-4)

What was Jonathan's plan? (v. 5-23)

What was Saul's response to Jonathan? (v. 24-33)

What happened between Jonathan and David? (v. 34-42)

Day 5: Read 1 Samuel 21

Why did David need Goliath's sword? (v. 1-9)

Why did David pretend insanity? (v. 10-15)

For Further Study

Key Verse: "Then David said to the Philistine, 'You come to me with a sword, with a spear, and with a javelin. But I come to you in the name of the Lord of hosts, the God of the armies of Israel, whom you have defied.' "

1 Samuel 17:45

Lesson 39

Overview

The Biblical account of David's life is both exciting to study and full of lessons that we can easily apply to our own walk of faith. We should keep in mind as we study David's life that God called David a man after His own heart (1 Samuel 13:14, Acts 13:22). It is nothing but helpful to our own Christian lives to study a man after God's own heart. We should all desire to have that kind of faith and devotion to God.

This lesson highlights the continued threats against David's life from King Saul. One of the many ways David showed his absolute faith in God's plan is that he continually spared Saul's life, even as others urged him to kill Saul. Certainly the entire kingdom would know that David acted in self-defense. But David refused to take matters into his own hands. He was not afraid to kill those who were the enemies of God and His people, as we saw in the account of Goliath and the Philistines. In these chapters we learn about many times that God used David to execute judgment on the ungodly. Remember that Israel would not have been dealing with these continued battles were it not for their own disobedience when they entered the Promised Land. So David was not afraid to stand up to his enemies; rather, he was so close to God that he knew when it was God's will to act and when it was not.

This is also a good time to consider the Psalms David wrote during this time in his life and throughout his lifetime. In those we see a glimpse into David's deep feelings about all that was happening to him. His trust in God did not mean that he did not have hard days and sometimes difficulty trusting. But he persevered and became a great example of a life dedicated to living for a loving, holy and wise God. If you have extra time this week, turn to Psalms and spend some time letting David's deepest feelings sink into your own heart and mind. Psalm 23, 9, and 38 are good places to start.

Lesson 39

Daily Bible Study

Day 1: Read 1 Samuel 22

Who was with David? (v. 1-5)

How did Ahimelech defend David? (v. 6-15)

What did Saul do? (v. 16-23)

Day 2: Read 1 Samuel 23

What happened at Keilah? (v. 1-13)

How did Jonathan encourage David? (v. 14-18)

Why did they call the Wilderness of Maon the Rock of Escape? (v. 19-29)

Day 3: Read 1 Samuel 24

Why was David upset over cutting Saul's robe? (v. 1-7)

What did David declare to Saul? (v. 8-15)

What did Saul declare to David? (v. 16-22)

_____

_____

Day 4: Read 1 Samuel 25

How are Abigail and Nabal described? (v. 1-3)

_____

What was David's request and Nabal's response? (v. 4-11)

_____

What was David's response? (v. 12-13)

_____

What did Nabal's servants do? (v. 14-17)

_____

What did Abigail do? (v. 18-22)

_____

_____

What did Abigail say to David? (v. 23-31)

_____

_____

What happened? (v. 32-44)

_____

Day 5: Read 1 Samuel 26

Why did David spare Saul's life? (v. 1-12)

_____

What did David want? (v. 13-25)

_____

_____

For Further Study

Key Verses: "Then Jonathan, Saul's son, arose and went to David in the woods and strengthened his hand in God. And he said to him, 'Do not fear, for the hand of Saul my father shall not find you. You shall be king over Israel and I shall be next to you. Even my father Saul knows that.' "

1 Samuel 23:16-17

Lesson 40

Overview

Since three of the chapters in this lesson are very short, some suggested Psalms are given to deepen the study. Psalms, mostly written by David, is a great book to read daily so that we can learn to pour our hearts out to God. David taught us to bring our deepest and darkest feelings to the throne of our loving heavenly Father.

This lesson concludes the book of 1 Samuel and also gives the account of the end of Saul's life. Saul's life is a tragic reminder of the importance of obeying God completely and yielding our own will to His. Saul made decisions based on what he wanted and when, rather than waiting for God's will. Just as David's life is a great example of how we should walk with God, Saul's life is a great example of the consequences of walking our own way. The entire nation of Israel, as well as many Christians today, tended to walk in the flesh rather than in the power of the Holy Spirit.

As you read each day, be sure to spend time pondering what God would speak to your own heart about the Old Testament accounts. These are interesting stories, but they are also meant to teach us about God's nature, man's nature, and what it means to live a life pleasing to God. It is sometimes easy to overlook or misinterpret the message that God has for our own heart as we study His Word. The Holy Spirit is our guide.

In this lesson we read the interesting story of how Saul consulted a medium (psychic) for guidance. God had already given specific commandments about such practices. And obviously if Saul had a right relationship with God, he would not have found himself in such a dismal place in his life. Try to imagine what this passage is teaching about consulting psychics for direction in life. Note the reaction of the medium to Samuel's appearance.

Lesson 40

Daily Bible Study

Day 1: Read 1 Samuel 27 (Psalm 34)

Why did David want to live with the Philistines? (v. 1-3)
_____
_____

Why did Achish believe David would always be loyal to him? (v. 4-12)
_____
_____

Day 2: Read 1 Samuel 28

Why was Saul afraid, and what did he do? (v. 1-7)
_____

What was Samuel's message to Saul? (v. 8-19)
_____
_____

Why did Saul not want to eat? (v. 20-25)
_____
_____

Day 3: Read 1 Samuel 29 (Psalm 57)

Why were the Philistine military leaders upset? (v. 1-5)
_____

Why did Achish make David go back? (v. 6-11)
_____
_____

Day 4: Read 1 Samuel 30

What happened at Ziklag? (v. 1-6)

_____
_____
_____

What was God's word to David? (v. 7-8)

_____
_____

How did the Egyptian slave help David? (v. 9-16)

_____
_____

Why were some of the men upset, and how did David handle it? (v. 17-25)

_____
_____

Where did David send some of the spoils? (v. 26-31)

_____
_____

Day 5: Read 1 Samuel 31　　　　　(Psalm 54)

How did Saul die? (v. 1-5)

_____
_____

What did the Philistines do? (v. 6-10)

_____
_____

What did the Israelites do? (v. 11-13)

_____
_____
_____
_____

For Further Study

Key Verses: "And the Lord has done for Himself as He spoke by me. For the Lord has torn the kingdom out of your hand and given it to your neighbor, David. Because you did not obey the voice of the Lord nor execute His fierce wrath upon Amalek, therefore the Lord has done this thing to you this day."

1 Samuel 28:17-18

Lesson 41

Overview

Second Samuel is the place where many people's knowledge of the Old Testament begins to get foggy. The main reason for this is that 2 Samuel is the place where God begins to give us more than one account of an event in order to teach us different aspects of the lesson He wants us to learn. For example, everything we have read so far in the Old Testament has been chronological, except for the book of Job. Remember that Job is grouped with the poetry books, but historically the events happened during the Genesis time period. But other than Job, all of the books we have studied have been in the order of the events.

After Saul's death at the end of 1 Samuel, there are many things happening in Israel at the same time. The books of Samuel, Kings and Chronicles begin to overlap in order to show all that God intended in His Word. The events of 2 Samuel are repeated in 1 Chronicles, and the two books of Kings are the same time period as 2 Chronicles. It will be easy to see as we study the main events that God was providing different perspectives to teach us different lessons, similar to the life of Jesus in the 4 gospels (Matthew, Mark, Luke and John). To further challenge us, the books of the prophets from Isaiah through Malachi are interspersed chronologically throughout 2 Samuel, Kings, Chronicles, Ezra, Nehemiah and Esther. This will all make sense as we study through these lessons.

This lesson begins with the Amalekite lying to David about killing Saul. We see the rocky beginning of David's reign as king of Israel, and we read about David's wives and sons. Keep in mind that it was customary in that day for a man to have multiple wives, especially men of high ranking. But it was never God's plan, and it caused much grief to go against God's plan for families.

Lesson 41

Daily Bible Study

Day 1: Read 2 Samuel 1

What did the Amalekite say, and was it true? (v. 1-10; see 1 Samuel 31:4 if you don't remember)

_____
_____

What two responses did David have? (v. 11-16)

_____
_____

What stands out to you about the Song of the Bow? (v. 17-27)

_____
_____

Day 2: Read 1 Chronicles 10

What additional information is given here about Saul? (v. 1-14)

_____
_____
_____
_____

Day 3: Read 2 Samuel 2

What happened next for David? (v. 1-7)

_____

Why did David bless the men of Jabesh Gilead? (also, v. 1-7)

_____
_____

Who was Ishbosheth? (v. 8-11)

_____
_____

What happened at the Field of Sharp Swords? (v. 12-17)

_____

Who were Joab and Abner, and why were they fighting? (v. 18-32)

Day 4: Read 2 Samuel 3

What was a notable problem in David's family (see overview)? (v. 1-5)

What happened between Abner and Ishbosheth? (v. 6-11)

What happened between Abner and David? (v. 12-21)

Why was Joab angry, and what did he do? (v. 22-27)

What was David's response? (v. 28-39)

Day 5: Read 2 Samuel 4 (Psalm 1)

Who was Mephibosheth? (v. 1-4)

Why did David have Rechab and Baanah executed? (v. 5-12)

For Further Study

Key Verse: "It happened after this that David inquired of the Lord, saying, 'Shall I go up to any of the cities of Judah?' And the Lord said to him, 'Go up.' David said, 'Where shall I go up?' And He said, 'To Hebron.' "

2 Samuel 2:1

Lesson 42

Overview

As we move deeper into 2 Samuel, we will see many chapters repeated in 1 Chronicles, while some events are given only in one book. Sometimes we will read both accounts, and sometimes we will simply note the corresponding chapter(s) in either 2 Samuel or 1 Chronicles. The books of Samuel are obviously named for the prophet and judge, Samuel, while the name of 1 and 2 Chronicles indicates the chronicles (accounts) of the kings of Israel and Judah. To further complicate things, David wrote most of the book of Psalms during this time period (1 and 2 Samuel and 1 Chronicles), so we will occasionally read or note a corresponding Psalm. It is very helpful to try to read Psalms along with this study. You could use the extra days of the week to fit in some Psalms, or you could read one or two chapters of Psalms along with the Samuel/Chronicles study. We will study Psalms and the poetry books later.

Hopefully you will notice significant differences between David and Saul as the first two kings of Israel. From the beginning of his reign, David was committed to doing exactly what God wanted him to do. This does not mean that David was perfect, but he was quick to repent when he sinned. 2 Samuel 6 is the difficult story of Uzzah's mistake. We see that the people, including David, did not bother to find out exactly how God wanted the Ark of the Covenant handled. God had given very specific instructions, and He showed them not to take His words lightly. This is a great lesson for us today as we seek to obey God's Word: obedience begins with actually knowing what God has said on the issues of our lives. 2 Timothy 2:15 instructs us: "Be diligent to present yourself approved to God, a worker who does not need to be ashamed, rightly dividing the word of truth." David and the entire kingdom of Israel had to learn the importance of finding out and following exactly what God says.

Lesson 42

Daily Bible Study

Day 1: Read 2 Samuel 5   (Compare 1 Chronicles 11, 12, 14)

How old was David when he became king, and how long did he reign? (v. 1-5)

How did David know God had established him as king? (v. 6-12)

What is a significant difference between Saul and David? (v. 13-25)

Day 2: Read 2 Samuel 6   (Compare 1 Chronicles 13, 15)

Why were David and the people so happy? (v. 1-5)

What happened to Uzzah and why? (v. 6-7)

What two emotions does David have? (v. 8-9)

Who was blessed, and why? (v. 10-11)

What did David do next, and how did he feel? (v. 12-15)

Why did Michal have no children? (v. 16-23)

Day 3: Read 1 Chronicles 15

Who would carry the ark, and why? (v. 1-3)
___

How did they know God's instructions? (v. 4-15)
___

Why did Michal despise David? (v. 16-29)
___

Day 4: Read 1 Chronicles 16   (and Psalm 105)

What were some of the responsibilities of the Levites? (v. 1-6)
___

What are some specific ways to praise God? (v. 7-24)
___

How did the people respond? (v. 25-36)
___

How and why was regular worship restored and maintained? (v. 37-43)
___

Day 5: Read 1 Chronicles 17   (Compare 2 Samuel 7)

What was Nathan's mistake? (v. 1-6)
___

What was God's message instead? (v. 7-15)
___

What was David's response? Write your favorite thoughts from David's prayer. (v. 16-27)
___

For Further Study

Key Verses: "So the priests and the Levites sanctified themselves to bring up the ark of the Lord God of Israel. And the children of the Levites bore the ark of God on their shoulders, by its poles, as Moses had commanded according to the word of the Lord."

           1 Chronicles 15:14-15

Lesson 43

Overview

This week's lesson will focus more on 2 Samuel, and we will notice that 2 Samuel provides more personal information about King David's life. We will read the story of Jonathan's son, Mephibosheth, who was first mentioned in Lesson 41, 2 Samuel 4. Note that this very special story is found only in 2 Samuel.

The story of David and Bathsheba is also found only in 2 Samuel. As you read, remember that in the beginning of his reign, David always went to battle with his army, as was the custom of kings. In 2 Samuel 11, David stayed home. No reason is given, but we see the tragic mistake David made as he was presumably not where he should have been. It might also be noted that Bathsheba was obviously in the wrong place as well, if her bath was noticeable from the balcony of a different house. David's sin led him into further sin as he tried to cover it up. He went from sexual sin to murder. We are not sure from the biblical record how much time passed, but we know David confessed and repented when the prophet, Nathan, confronted him. Psalm 51 is David's prayer of repentance and remorse. We also have a remarkable verse about David's belief in eternal life, and the salvation of his young son.

As you come to enjoy digging deeper into God's Word, try to expand your study from five days per week to every single day. There are great blessings for us as we soak our minds and hearts in God's Word. The key verses are just suggestions, with plenty of room on the "For Further Study" pages to write other verses or passages that may stand out to you. For the extra days of study, you might catch up on any particularly long chapters, or you may turn to Psalms and/or Proverbs for daily inspiration. These can be read according to the date; for example, read Proverbs 5 on the 5th day of the month. We will study Psalms, Proverbs, and the other poetry books at the end of the study.

Lesson 43

Daily Bible Study

Day 1: Read 2 Samuel 8   **(Compare 1 Chronicles 18)**

What were some specific victories for David, and what was God's view? (v. 1-6)

How did the rulers of the surrounding nations view David? (v. 7-10)

Describe David's administration. (v. 11-18)

Day 2: Read 2 Samuel 9

What did David want to do and why? (v. 1-4)

What was Mephibosheth's reaction? (v. 5-8)

What did David do for Mephibosheth? (v. 9-13)

Day 3: Read 2 Samuel 10   **(Compare 1 Chronicles 19)**

What was Hanun's mistake? (v. 1-4)

What was David's response? (v. 5-10)

What was the result? (v. 11-19)

Day 4: Read 2 Samuel 11

What was David's mistake? (v. 1-5)

What was David's response? (v. 6-8)

What kind of man was Uriah? (v. 9-11)

What happened to Uriah? (v. 12-17)

Why was Joab worried? (v. 18-22)

What happened next, and how did God feel? (v. 23-27)

Day 5: Read 2 Samuel 12   (and Psalm 51)

What was the point of Nathan's story? (v. 1-4)

What would be the result of David's sin? (v. 5-15)

Describe David's feelings about his child's illness and death. (v. 15-23)

How did God and Nathan feel toward Solomon? (v. 24-31)

For Further Study

Key Verses: "Be of good courage, and let us be strong for our people and for the cities of our God. And may the Lord do what is good in His sight."

2 Samuel 10:12 **and** 1 Chronicles 19:13

Lesson 44

Overview

2 Samuel 13-20 contains accounts of tragedies within David's family. These accounts are not mentioned at all in 1 Chronicles. The reading and studying of these accounts are difficult for many reasons. Many people are uncomfortable with the idea that a man like David, called "a man after God's own heart" by God Himself, could have such failures in his personal life. And since God did not specifically mention David's sin of polygamy (marrying multiple wives), we wonder what sins we are embracing in our culture that we are not even noticing, but that are displeasing to God. We will skip the reading of these chapters for this study, but as always, they are equally important in God's Word. So, read them if you can. We will move on in the overview of David's reign.

Here is a reminder that the different accounts in 2 Samuel and 1 Chronicles are worth noting. Notice also that 2 Samuel 22 is the same as Psalm 18. Keep in mind that these books of the Bible are deeply interconnected. It is very worthwhile to study this section of scripture and learn how it all fits together. As always, there are deep lessons for us when we dig into God's Word.

The story of the Gibeonites is mentioned in both accounts. This is an interesting lesson about the importance God puts on keeping the promises we make. The Gibeonites tricked Joshua into making a treaty with them, and later Saul dealt harshly with them. The famine was God's punishment, all those years later, for Saul's violating the treaty. Even though the treaty was originally a mistake, God still meant them to keep their word. As always, as you read these stories, ask God to show you what areas of your life need to be made pure and right before Him.

2 Samuel ends with the tragic story of David's census. It reminds us that our personal sins often have consequences for others.

Lesson 44

Daily Bible Study

Day 1: Read 2 Samuel 21   (Compare 1 Chronicles 20)

Why did God cause a famine? (v. 1-2; compare Joshua 9)
_____
_____

What did the Gibeonites ask for? (v. 3-6)
_____
_____

Who was spared and why? (v. 7)
_____
_____

What happened with the famine? (v. 8-14)
_____
_____

Why do you think Israel had so much trouble with the Philistines? (v. 15-22; compare Joshua 13:13 and Judges 3:1-6)
_____
_____

Day 2: Read 2 Samuel 22   (and Psalm 18)

Write out your favorite thoughts from this chapter.
_____
_____
_____

Day 3: Read 2 Samuel 23

What is the main point of David's last words? (v. 1-7)
_____
_____

Why would David not drink the water? (v. 8-17)
_____
_____

Although lists of names can be difficult, try to pick out a few that stand out to you. (v. 18-39; expanded list in 1 Chronicles 11)

Day 4: Read 2 Samuel 24   (Compare 1 Chronicles 21)

How did Joab feel about David's census? (v. 1-4)

Note the borders of Israel (still a big issue today). How many fighting men were there? (v. 5-9)

How did David feel after the census? (v. 10)

Why did David choose the 3 day plague? (v. 11-14)

What did God command? (v. 15-19)

Why did David not accept Araunah's offer? (v. 20-25)

Day 5: Read 1 Chronicles 22

What did David want Solomon to do? (v. 1-6)

Why did God allow Solomon and not David to build the temple? (v. 7-10)

What was the main focus of David's instructions to Solomon? (v. 11-19)

(Interesting to note: try to find out the value of a talent of gold in today's currency, and calculate the material value of the temple.)

For Further Study

Key Verses: "And he said: 'The Lord is my rock and my fortress and my deliverer; the God of my strength, in whom I will trust; my shield and the horn of my salvation; my stronghold and my refuge; my Savior, You save me from violence. I will call upon the Lord, who is worthy to be praised; so shall I be saved from my enemies.' "

2 Samuel 22:2-4 **and** Psalm 18:2-3

Lesson 45

Overview

This week we begin the books of the Kings. Notice that just as 2 Samuel and 1 Chronicles had similar accounts of the same time period, 1 and 2 Kings are similar to 2 Chronicles in that they cover the same time period. As we have noted, this is where the study of the Old Testament can be confusing if read casually, but deeper study and comparison bring out the richness God provides in this part of His Word. And although we will not read every chapter in this overview, every chapter is important and is worth the time to read and study.

We will also conclude 1 Chronicles this week, skipping the long lists of names in 1 Chronicles 23-27. But one thing to remember about these lists of names is that God is interested in individuals as well as nations. 1 Chronicles concludes with David's specific instructions to Solomon about the temple, which were given publicly for the sake of Israel and for Solomon. We will also read about the end of David's reign. 1 Kings begins with the rocky start to Solomon's reign, which is not mentioned in the Chronicles.

Next we focus on Solomon's reign, recorded in both 2 Chronicles and 1 Kings. Solomon's life has many interesting and thought-provoking components. Keep in mind that Solomon wrote the books of Proverbs, Ecclesiastes and Song of Solomon. It will be helpful to your study to spend some time in those books while you study Solomon's reign over Israel. We will read the fascinating account of God's offering to Solomon anything he wanted, and Solomon's request.

Nothing is mentioned in Kings and Chronicles about God's rules for kings found in Deuteronomy 17:14-20, but Solomon certainly violated those. We note from 1 Kings 3:3 that Solomon loved the Lord. God was pleased with Solomon as well, and blessed his reign.

Lesson 45

Daily Bible Study

Day 1: Read 1 Chronicles 28

What message did David have for Israel? (v. 1-7)

What message did David have for Solomon? (v. 8-10)

How did David know the specifics of the temple building plans? (v. 11-19)

What further word did David have for Solomon? (v. 20-21)

Day 2: Read 1 Chronicles 29

What was the specific reason for rejoicing? (v. 1-9)

What were some of the things David prayed for? (v. 10-19)

What stands out to you about Solomon becoming king? (v. 20-30)

Day 3: Read 1 Kings 3   **(Compare 2 Chronicles 1)**

How did Solomon feel towards God? (v. 1-4)

What did God offer, and what was Solomon's response? (v. 5-9)

What was God's response? (v. 10-15)

How did Solomon show wisdom? (v. 16-28)

Day 4: Read 2 Chronicles 2   (Compare 1 Kings 5)

What did Solomon request of Hiram and why? (v. 1-10)

What was Hiram's response? (v. 11-18)

(Are there any additional facts that stand out in 1 Kings 5?)

Day 5: Read 2 Chronicles 3   (Compare 1 Kings 6)

What stands out first to you about the temple construction? (v. 1-9)

Describe the Most Holy Place. (v. 10-17)

Note any other interesting thoughts from 1 Kings 6.

Any extra time this week could be spent comparing New Testament passages such as Hebrews 9 and 1 Corinthians 6:19.

For Further Study

Key Verse: "As for you, my son, Solomon, know the God of your father, and serve Him with a loyal heart and with a willing mind; for the Lord searches all hearts and understands all the intent of the thoughts. If you seek Him, He will be found by you; but if you forsake Him, He will cast you off forever."

1 Chronicles 28:9

Lesson 46

Overview

If you are able to spend time comparing the different accounts in Kings and Chronicles, it will add so much richness to your study. It will also add to your study to read some of Solomon's other writings (Proverbs, Song of Solomon and Ecclesiastes) along with the accounts of his reign as king of Israel. Keep in mind that King Saul reigned for forty years; David reigned for forty years, and we see in this lesson that Solomon reigned for forty years. Those are the first three kings of Israel, and the only kings who reigned over the united kingdom of Israel. We will study the tragic dividing of Israel in the next lesson.

Notice that 2 Chronicles 5, 6, and 7 are the same as 1 Kings 8. 2 Chronicles 4 and 1 Kings 7 give us more details on the temple furnishings, although we will not read those chapters in this study. Take time to look over them if you can. The details of the splendor of the temple building and furnishings are amazing to imagine. As has been mentioned, it is very interesting to look up the weight of a talent of gold or silver and calculate the monetary value of the building materials. This would be the first of several temples that would be constructed, plundered by enemies, torn down and rebuilt. Later we will read how Nebuchadnezzar took all of these temple treasures, but 70 years after that Cyrus sent them all back with the Jews who had been captured and exiled when they returned.

Solomon's dedication speech and prayer are very inspiring. God's second appearance to Solomon is in both accounts as well.

One reason for comparing the two accounts is that some important truths are mentioned in only one of the books. For example, 1 Kings 11 gives us the important account of specifically how Solomon's heart was turned from God, but those details are not found in Chronicles.

Lesson 46

Daily Bible Study

Day 1: Read 2 Chronicles 5   (Compare 1 Kings 7:51-8:11)

How was Solomon's moving of the ark different from David's? (v. 1-5; compare 2 Samuel 6:3-7)

Describe the cherubim and the placement of the ark. (v. 6-10)

How did God show His presence? (v. 11-14)

Day 2: Read 2 Chronicles 6   (Compare 1 Kings 8:12-53)

What did Solomon testify before the people? (v. 1-11)

What would be the results of sin in Israel? (v. 12-31)

What did Solomon's prophetic prayer suggest would happen to Israel if they sinned against God? (v. 32-42)

Day 3: Read 2 Chronicles 7   (Compare 1 Kings 8:54-9:9)

How was the temple dedicated? (v. 1-5)

How long did the celebration last? (v. 6-11)

What was God's second message to Solomon? (v. 12-22)

_____

Day 4: Read 1 Kings 10   (Compare 2 Chronicles 9)

Why did the Queen of Sheba (modern day Yemen) visit Solomon and what was her response? (v. 1-13)

_____

How did God describe Solomon's wealth and wisdom? (v. 14-23)

_____

How did Solomon's wealth impact Jerusalem's economy? (v. 24-29)

_____

(Notice the horses from Egypt again.)

Day 5: Read 1 Kings 11

How was Solomon's heart turned away from God? (v. 1-8)

_____

What was God's response? (v. 9-13)

_____

What trouble did Solomon have? (v. 14-25)

_____

What was Abijah's message to Jeroboam? (v. 26-43)

_____

Be sure to try to read some of Solomon's personal writings in Proverbs, Song of Solomon and Ecclesiastes.

For Further Study

Key Verse: "If My people, who are called by My name will humble themselves, and pray and seek My face, and turn from their wicked ways, then I will hear from heaven, and will forgive their sin and heal their land."

1 Chronicles 7:14

_____
_____
_____
_____
_____
_____
_____
_____
_____
_____
_____
_____
_____
_____
_____
_____
_____
_____
_____
_____
_____
_____
_____
_____
_____

Lesson 47

Overview

This lesson gives us the heartbreaking details of how the kingdom of Israel was torn apart by one young man's foolish actions. The young man was Solomon's son, Rehoboam, who became king after Solomon. Israel was arguably the most respected nation in the world after the 80 years of David's and Solomon's reigns. In Lesson 46 we read about the message God had given Jeroboam about this (1 Kings 11:26-40).

There are many lessons for our lives in these accounts. We should first consider where we get advice when we have decisions to make. Do we seek Godly counsel from His Word and from more mature believers? Or do we find someone who will agree with what we really want to do? We are reminded that often our decisions affect others as well, as we have seen throughout our Old Testament study. Certainly Rehoboam's foolish decision had far-reaching consequences for himself, his family (particularly his sons, grandsons, etc., who ascended the throne after him), and the entire nation of Israel for hundreds of years.

Another important lesson is shown in God's prophetic message to Jeroboam. We are reminded that nothing that happens catches God off-guard. He already knows what will happen in every situation. That knowledge should cause us to trust Him more deeply, since we can rest assured that even when we make bad decisions He is there ready to restore us when we turn back to Him. He offered that hope to Israel, and He continues to offer hope to us today.

Comparing the accounts throughout Kings and Chronicles gives us a clearer picture of how God works. It is definitely worth the extra effort to learn more about His ways. Be sure to notice the difference between learning the truths presented in the Word and haphazardly applying scripture to suit ourselves.

Lesson 47

Daily Bible Study

Day 1: Read 2 Chronicles 10 (Compare 1 Kings 12:1-20)

What advice did the elders give to Rehoboam? (v. 1-7)
___
___

What advice did the young men give? (v. 8-11)
___
___

Which advice did Rehoboam take, and what was the result? (v. 12-19)
___
___

Day 2: Read 2 Chronicles 11 (Compare 1 Kings 12:21-33)

What was Shemaiah's message to Rehoboam, and what was the result? (v. 1-4)
___
___

Why did Rehoboam fortify the cities? (v. 5-12)
___
___

How did Judah become stronger? (v. 13-17)
___
___

Whom did Rehoboam intend to become king after himself? (v. 18-23)
___
___

Day 3: Read 1 Kings 13 (no Chronicles correlation)

Why did God send this man to Jeroboam? (v. 1-10)
___

What mistake did the "man of God" make? (v. 11-19)

How did the old prophet respond? (v. 20-34)

Day 4: Read 1 Kings 14   **(Compare 2 Chronicles 12)**

Why did Jeroboam's son die? (v. 1-18)

How did Rehoboam's reign turn out? (v. 19-31)

Day 5: Read 2 Chronicles 13   **(Compare 1 Kings 15:1-8)**

What did Abijah say to Jeroboam and to Israel? (v. 1-12)

Who prevailed in this battle? (v. 13-22)

Comparing 1 Kings 15:1-8, was Abijah really loyal to God?

*Reminder: Psalms (written mostly by David), Proverbs, Song of Solomon and Ecclesiastes (written by Solomon) were being written and compiled during the time of Samuel, Kings and Chronicles. We will study these books, known as the poetry books, at the end of the Old Testament study.

For Further Study

Key Verses: "Nevertheless for David's sake the Lord his God gave him a lamp in Jerusalem, by setting up his son after him and by establishing Jerusalem; because David did what was right in the eyes of the Lord, and had not turned aside from anything that He commanded him all the days of his life, except in the matter of Uriah the Hittite."

1 Kings 15:4-5

Lesson 48

Overview

As we progress through Kings and Chronicles, we should be very careful to note how the devotion of the kings to God had a direct effect on the people they ruled. You will notice that not a single king of the northern kingdom of Israel was devoted to God. In fact, most of them were compared to Jereboam in their wickedness for many generations. In the southern kingdom of Judah there were some good kings wholly devoted to God, but there were mostly bad kings who led the people to worship idols.

Also noteworthy is the fact that there was always found at least one true prophet of God in even the most evil times in both Israel and Judah. There were also false prophets willing to say just what an evil king or the ungodly people wanted to hear in every generation. That is a particular lesson for us: how can we know the difference between a prophet who is truly representing God's Word and one who is leading people away from God? The answer for us is found in God's Word itself. We have the benefit and unspeakable privilege of having God's complete Word available to us to read and study. We even have the specific command in 2 Timothy 2:15 to study God's Word in order not to be ashamed. The people of the Old Testament were not without counsel as well, since the books of Moses also gave them instruction on how to know a true prophet (Deuteronomy 18:15-22).

As we continue to compare and contrast the two accounts of this period of history, we notice that Chronicles begins to give more details about the southern kingdom of Judah, while Kings gives more details about the northern kingdom of Israel. There will still be some overlap, but we will begin to see more accounts given in only one place or the other. Ask God for sensitivity to see the lessons He has for you personally and avoid applying scripture haphazardly to modern situations.

Lesson 48

Daily Bible Study

Day 1: Read 2 Chronicles 14

In what specific ways did King Asa bring Judah back to true worship of God? (v. 1-5)

_____

_____

Describe Asa's military accomplishments. (v. 6-8)

_____

_____

Specifically how did Asa's army defeat the Ethiopians? (v. 9-15)

_____

(Compare Psalm 147:10-11 and Psalm 33:16-18. How did Asa's prayer reflect this principle?)

Day 2: Read 2 Chronicles 15   (1 Kings 15:9-15)

What encouragement did Azariah give to King Asa and Judah? (v. 1-7)

_____

Why did some people move from Israel to Judah? (v. 8-10)

_____

_____

What were the specifics of their renewed commitment to God? (v. 11-15)

_____

_____

What other things did Asa do to prove his commitment to God? (v. 16-19)

_____

_____

Day 3: Read 2 Chronicles 16   (1 Kings 15:16-34)

Why did Asa make a treaty with Syria? (v. 1-6)

_____

What was Hanani's message to Asa, and what was Asa's response? (v. 7-10)

How did Asa's reign end? (v. 11-14)

Why do you think Asa's faith in God failed?

From 1 Kings, how was Israel doing during this time?

Day 4: Read 1 Kings 16

What did Jehu say about Baasha? (v. 1-7)

Describe Elah's, Zimri's and Omri's reigns. (v. 8-28)

What particularly terrible thing did Ahab do? (v. 29-34)

Day 5: Read 2 Chronicles 17

In what specific ways did Jehoshaphat honor God, and what was God's response? (v. 1-6)

What did Jehoshaphat do with God's Word? (v. 7-10)

How did the other nations view Jehoshaphat? (v. 11-19)

For Further Study

Key Verse: "And Asa cried out to the Lord his God, and said, 'Lord, it is nothing for You to help, whether with many or with those who have no power; help us, O Lord our God, for we rest on You, and in Your name we go against this multitude. O Lord, You are our God; do not let man prevail against You!'"

2 Chronicles 14:11

Lesson 49

Overview

This lesson begins the immensely valuable account of the great prophet Elijah. We see God bringing Elijah on the scene of Israel's stage as the evil King Ahab is in power. Ahab's reign over Israel corresponds with King Asa and his son King Jehoshaphat in Judah. The next lesson will pick back up with what is happening during this time in Judah. This week we will concentrate on Israel and Elijah. As always, ask God to help you know what He would teach you through this powerful study of a great servant of God.

We are still in the history portion of the Old Testament. The poetry books and the books of the prophets follow. But as we have already seen, the poetry books were written during the time period of the books of Samuel, Kings and Chronicles. We will also see that most of the prophets lived during these times as well. We will soon begin to read them in the chronology of this time period. We should think about that as we read names of prophets in these accounts and consider what their prophecies concerned. For example, in this lesson a prophet named Obadiah is mentioned. Most Bible scholars do not believe this is the same Obadiah who wrote the Old Testament book of Obadiah, although obviously they were both prophets of God. But the book of Obadiah was written to the southern kingdom of Judah, while this prophet Obadiah lived in the northern kingdom of Israel. Certainly a prophet from Israel could prophesy about Judah, and that may be the case here, but we cannot be certain of that. For that reason, we will not assume they are the same person. We will wait to read the book of Obadiah until a little later in our study.

These are exciting chapters as we see God use the prophet Elijah to remind Israel that they must serve the only true God. We also see that even a powerful man of God like Elijah experienced times of discouragement, but God restores.

Lesson 49

Daily Bible Study

Day 1: Read 1 Kings 17

What was Elijah's message to Ahab? (v. 1)

How did God provide for Elijah? (v. 2-7)

Describe the miracle of the widow's flour and oil. (v. 8-16)

Describe the miracle of the widow's son. In verse 24, why do you think she didn't have true faith in God before? (v. 17-24)

Day 2: Read 1 Kings 18

What was remarkable about Obadiah? (v. 1-6)

Why was Obadiah afraid? (v. 7-14)

What was Elijah's message to Ahab? (v. 15-19)

What was Elijah's message to the people? (v. 20-21)

Describe the altar miracle. (v. 22-40)

How many times did the servant look for rain? (v. 41-46)

Day 3: Read 1 Kings 19

What was Jezebel's threat and Elijah's response? (v. 1-4)

What did God do for Elijah? (v. 5-8)

How did God reveal Himself to Elijah? (v. 9-13)

What was God's message to Elijah? (v. 14-18)

What happened with Elisha? (v. 19-21)

Day 4: Read 1 Kings 20

How did Ahab defeat the Syrians this time? (v. 1-22)

Why did God deliver Israel again from Syria? (v. 23-30)

What was God's response to Ahab's treaty with Syria? (v. 31-43)

Day 5: Read 1 Kings 21

Why did Naboth refuse to sell his vineyard? (v. 1-3)

How did Jezebel get Naboth's vineyard for Ahab? (v. 4-16)

What was God's message to Ahab? (v. 17-26)

How did Ahab respond? How did God respond? (v. 27-29)

For Further Study

Key Verse: "And Elijah came to all the people, and said, 'How long will you falter between two opinions? If the Lord is God, follow Him; but if Baal, follow him.' But the people answered him not a word."

1 Kings 18:21

Lesson 50

Overview

Meanwhile, back in Judah, King Jehoshaphat is still ruling, but he allies himself with Israel through the marriage of his son Jehoram to Athaliah, daughter of Ahab and Jezebel. We will study more about them in later chapters, but it should already be clear that this was not a wise decision for King Jehoshaphat. Nevertheless, Jehoshaphat is a Godly king who leads Judah in true worship of God. Notice that the account of Micaiah's prophecy is given in both 1 Kings 22 and 2 Chronicles 18, even though most of what we are studying is given in only one of these books. Notice what Micaiah first tells Ahab and Jehoshaphat. How often do we also miss God's word to us because we just do not want to hear it? But at least Ahab recognized that Micaiah had not given him the true word of the Lord, and he did ask for it.

The next chapters give us the wonderful lessons of King Jehoshaphat's reign. He followed the example of godliness of his father, King Asa, and Judah was blessed for it. There are many great lessons for our own Christian lives as we study the strengths and weaknesses of these kings. We see God blessing their faithfulness and allowing judgment when they turn away. How many hardships do we face because we are unfaithful?

Before we continue in Chronicles with the kings of Judah, we will turn back (chronologically) and catch up with the happenings in Israel. Ahab has died in battle as Micaiah had prophesied, and his son Ahaziah rules next. We get to read the exciting account of Elijah's ascension to Heaven. We only know of two men who have gone to Heaven without dying. Do you remember the other one? After Elijah goes to Heaven in the fiery chariot, we go right into the life of Elisha, servant of Elijah. The miracles of Elisha should always strengthen our own faith as we see God's provision time after time. Notice that God provides for us even when we are not expecting it.

Lesson 50

Daily Bible Study

Day 1: Read 2 Chronicles 18   (1 Kings 22)

Why was Jehoshaphat not pleased with the prophets in Israel? (v. 1-6)
___
___

What did Micaiah prophesy? Also, what stands out to you about Micaiah? (v. 7-27)
___
___

How did Ahab die? (v. 28-34)
___
___

Day 2: Read 2 Chronicles 19

What did God say about Jehoshaphat through Jehu? (v. 1-3)
___
___

What message did Jehoshaphat have for the judges? (v. 4-7)
___
___

What were Jehoshaphat's priorities in the governing of Judah? (v. 8-11)
___
___

Day 3: Read 2 Chronicles 20

Why was Jehoshaphat afraid? (v. 1-12)
___
___

Describe Jahaziel's prophecy. (v. 13-19)
___
___

How were Judah's enemies defeated? (v. 20-30)

What mistakes did Jehoshaphat make? (v. 31-37)

Day 4: Read 2 Kings 1

What happened to Ahaziah, and what did he do? (v. 1-2)

What was Elijah's message to Ahaziah? (v. 3-8)

Why was the third captain spared? (v. 9-15)

What happened? (v. 16-18)

Day 5: Read 2 Kings 2

Why did Elisha not want to leave Elijah? (v. 1-6)

What happened to the Jordan River? (v. 7-8)

What happened to Elijah? (v. 9-13)

What did the sons of the prophets do? (v. 14-18)

Describe these miracles. (v. 19-25)

For Further Study

Key Verse: " 'You will not need to fight in this battle. Position yourselves, stand still and see the salvation of the Lord, who is with you, O Judah and Jerusalem!' Do not fear or be dismayed; tomorrow go out against them, for the Lord is with you."

2 Chronicles 20:17

Lesson 51

Overview

The chapters in this lesson are arguably some of the most encouraging and amazing in the entire Bible. Every chapter in this lesson shows us how abundantly God provides for His people and how surprising those miracles of provision can be. God uses His servant Elisha to proclaim these provisions.

In 2 Kings 3 we read about digging ditches to contain the miraculous waters of survival and blessing. Chapter 4 is the famous story of collecting containers for the oil of abundance. Then a miraculous son is miraculously raised from the dead. In chapter 5 leprosy is healed in a surprising and unpleasant way, and leprosy is given to a dishonest servant. Chapter 6 gives us the floating ax head; a servant's eyes are opened, and the whole Syrian army is blinded. Then in chapter 7 a different Syrian army hears miraculous sounds that cause them to run for their lives and provides the Israelites with all they need. A doubter is trampled because of the excitement of the people over the bountiful provision.

All of these accounts show us yet another set of reasons to study the great stories of the Old Testament and understand their context. As we read accounts of God's provision for entire armies and for one simple widow, we are reminded of that great truth found in Ephesians 3:20-21: "Now to Him who is able to do exceedingly abundantly above all that we ask or think, according to the power that works in us, to Him be glory in the church by Christ Jesus to all generations, forever and ever. Amen." We don't even know what could be "above all that we ask or think" if we haven't even read the accounts God has given us. The believers in Ephesus presumably knew those accounts, and we should too.

Keeping the kings of Israel and Judah straight in our minds is helpful at this point. We will review in the next lesson.

Lesson 51

Daily Bible Study

Day 1: Read 2 Kings 3

What kind of king was Ahab's son, Jehoram? (v. 1-3)

What was the problem for the armies? (v. 4-10)

What did Jehoshaphat do? (v. 11-13)

What was Elisha's message, and what was the outcome? (v. 14-27)

Day 2: Read 2 Kings 4

Describe this miracle. (v. 1-7)

Why did Elisha want to bless the Shunammite woman, and how did he bless her? (v. 8-17)

What happened to the son? (v. 18-37)

What happened to the stew? (v. 38-41)

Why was the servant upset, and what happened? (v. 42-44)

Day 3: Read 2 Kings 5

Who was Naaman, and what was wrong with him? (v. 1)
_____

Why was the king upset? (v. 2-7)
_____

Why was Naaman angry? (v. 8-12)
_____
_____

What happened? (v. 13-19)
_____

Why did Gehazi get leprosy? (v. 20-27)
_____

Day 4: Read 2 Kings 6

Why did the ax head float? (v. 1-7)
_____

How was Elisha troubling the king of Syria? (v. 8-12)
_____

How were the Syrian raiders defeated? (v. 13-23)
_____
_____

Why did God allow this terrible siege? (v. 24-33)
_____

Day 5: Read 2 Kings 7

What was Elisha's response? (v. 1-3)
_____

Why did the Syrian army flee? (v. 4-7)
_____

What was the king of Israel afraid of? (v. 8-12)
_____

How was Elisha's prophecy fulfilled? (v. 13-20)
_____
_____

For Further Study

Key Verse: "And Elisha prayed, and said, 'Lord, I pray, open his eyes that he may see.' Then the Lord opened the eyes of the young man and he saw. And behold, the mountain was full of horses and chariots of fire all around Elisha."

2 Kings 6:17

Lesson 52

Overview

The chapters in these lessons are very exciting for those who love history, but the lessons can become challenging and even confusing without careful study. We should remind ourselves again of the need to apply ourselves to the study of scripture (2 Timothy 2:15). The study of God's dealing with His people teaches us many great truths about our heavenly Father and also ourselves. These great truths can provide us with sound wisdom and greater faith. Just as we become better citizens of our country through the study of where we have been as a nation, so we become more useful to God's kingdom through understanding more of the nature of our great God and King. It changes our whole perspective to study the lives of people who served or didn't serve God and how they went wrong or right. Without knowledge we flounder in a sea of ignorance where our enemy the devil can attack us in the exact same ways he attacked our forebears. Let us not become weary in the study of God's Word. What a privilege to live in a time and place where we have the revealed Word of God. Let us make the most of the opportunity to learn more of Him.

Keeping the kings of Israel and Judah straight is a challenge in itself. With Jehoshaphat allowing his son to marry the daughter of Ahab and Jezebel and many of the kings having the same or similar names, it can easily get confusing. It is important to remember that none of the kings of Israel were God-fearing, while some of the kings of Judah did turn the hearts of the people back to true worship of God. Sometimes even the good kings did not completely get rid of all idol-worship, which became the ultimate un-doing of both Israel and Judah.

We will begin to read the prophets who wrote during the times of the kings as well. So get ready to add more books to the study! To understand how the books of prophecy fit into the Old Testament narrative gives a richness to their messages.

Lesson 52
Daily Bible Study

Day 1: Read 2 Kings 8

How did God bless the Shunammite woman's obedience? (v. 1-6)

What happened to the king of Syria and why do you think God included this portion of Syrian history? (v. 7-15)

Who became king in Judah, and was he a good king? (v. 16-24)

Who was Ahaziah's mother and grandfathers? (v. 25-29)

Day 2: Read 2 Chronicles 21   (2 Kings 9, 10)

What new information is given about Jehoram of Judah? (v. 1-7)

What had Elijah prophesied about Jehoram? (v. 8-15)

Why was no one sad when Jehoram died? (v. 16-20)

Day 3: Read 2 Chronicles 22   (2 Kings 11)

What happened to Ahaziah? (v. 1-9)

Who was Athaliah, and what did she do? (v. 10)

Who was Joash, and how was he saved? (v. 11-12)

Day 4: Read 2 Chronicles 23   (2 Kings 11)

Who was Jehoiada, and what did he do? (v. 1-11)

What happened to Queen Athaliah? (v. 12-21)

Day 5: Read 2 Chronicles 24   (2 Kings 12)

What remarkable fact about Joash is given in verse 1?

Give specific evidence for the kind of man and king Joash was. (v. 2-4)

What did Joash do to show devotion to God? (v. 5-14)

What happened after Jehoiada died? (v. 15-22)

What happened to Joash and why? (v. 23-27)

For Further Study

Key Verse: "Yet the Lord would not destroy Judah, for the sake of His servant David, as He promised him to give a lamp to him and his sons forever."

2 Kings 8:19

Lesson 53

Overview

It is time to begin to incorporate some of the books of the prophets found later in the Old Testament into our study. As we have mentioned, the study of the kings and prophets is challenging, and most people never take the time to sort it all out. But the rewards of studying carefully this section of the Bible are immeasurable.

There are many differing opinions among Bible scholars over the exact dates of many of the books of the prophets. The first prophet that we will read, Obadiah, is an example. Some scholars place the writings of Obadiah earlier and some later. Obadiah prophesies about judgment on Edom, the descendants of Esau, who continually fought against the Israelites. Remember the promise God made to Abraham in Genesis about those who treat His people well and those who curse His people (Genesis 12:3). God's chosen people came from Abraham through Isaac and Jacob. Esau's descendants did not follow God and treated the Israelites badly. Obadiah prophesies their demise. The debates over the timing of the writings are interesting to read, but no matter when the books were written, they still show the omniscience (knowledge) and omnipotence (power) of our great God. Reading these prophecies and recognizing how precisely they were fulfilled gives even more depth to our faith and our praise of God.

Many of the prophecies in the Old Testament were fulfilled during the Old Testament times, many more in New Testament times, and many are still to be fulfilled. In this lesson we will read Obadiah's and Joel's prophecies which match the section of Kings and Chronicles that we are studying. Notice that the prophets were speaking God's Word to particular people in particular situations. It is important to understand which messages of the prophets were only for those generations.

Lesson 53

Daily Bible Study

Day 1: Read Obadiah

What was God's message to Edom? (v. 1-9)

Why would Edom be punished? (v. 10-16)

What did God promise Israel? (v. 17-21)

Day 2: Read Joel 1

How did Joel describe the land? (v. 1-12)

What did Joel want the priests to do and why? (v. 13-20)

Day 3: Read Joel 2

How did Joel describe the "day of the Lord"? (v. 1-11)

What did Joel ask the people to do? (v. 12-17)

What promises did God give? (v. 18-27)

What are some evidences of God's Spirit being poured out? (v. 28-32)

Day 4: Read Joel 3

How did Israel's enemies oppress them? (v. 1-6)

What are some ways God encouraged His people? (v. 7-17)

How will God bless His people? (v. 18-21)

Day 5: Read 2 Kings 13

Why did God deliver Israel from Syria this time? (v. 1-9)

Compare and contrast King Joash of Judah (2 Kings 12) and King Joash (Jehoash in some translations) of Israel. (v. 10-13)

Why was Elisha angry with Joash? (v. 14-19)

What remarkable miracle happened at Elisha's tomb, and what did it show? (v. 20-21)

How many times did Joash defeat Syria, and why is that remarkable? (v. 22-25)

For Further Study

Key Verses: " 'Now therefore,' says the Lord, 'Turn to Me with all your heart, with fasting, with weeping, and with mourning.' So rend your heart, and not your garments; return to the Lord your God, for He is gracious and merciful, slow to anger, and of great kindness; and He relents from doing harm."

Joel 2:12-13

Lesson 54

Overview

We will continue to connect the reading of the prophets to the Kings and Chronicles narratives. As we have mentioned before, there is interesting debate over the exact placement of many of the books of the prophets. It is useful to study several different views of chronology as you read these wonderful books. This study is one view; the helps section in the back has suggestions for other views.

Jonah is one of the more well-known stories in the Old Testament, as well as one of the more controversial accounts. Did Jonah actually spend three days in the belly of a fish? This is a good place to reevaluate your own view of scripture. Is it true? Is it all true? Is it really God's Word? If you have read this far, it would take a great amount of faith in human reasoning to conclude that the Bible is not indeed God's Holy Word.

Sometimes when we read Bible stories like Jonah's that are already familiar to us, it is easy to skim or not to read as carefully. Always take time to read carefully; God's Word is "the way of truth" (Psalm 119:30), and He always has something new to teach us (Hebrews 4:12). Look carefully into the lessons of Jonah and you may be surprised by what God shows you about your own level of obedience as well as your attitude.

Keep in mind that Jonah was a prophet in Israel, the northern kingdom, and Assyria was one of their worst enemies. Nineveh was the capital of Assyria, and we will read in the next few chapters of Kings and Chronicles about how Assyria ultimately defeated Israel and carried them away captive. This information gives us a little more insight into why Jonah not only did not want to preach salvation to these people, but why he really did not want them to be saved at all. He wanted God to destroy them. Ask God to give you greater insight into your own attitude about praying for your enemies.

Lesson 54

Daily Bible Study

Day 1: Read 2 Chronicles 25 (2 Kings 14)

Describe Amaziah's relationship to God. (v. 1-4)
___
___

How did Amaziah demonstrate a divided heart (or hypocrisy in his loyalty to God)? (v. 5-16)
___
___

What did Amaziah lose? (v. 17-28)
___
___

Day 2: Read Jonah 1

What did God tell Jonah to do, and what did Jonah do? (v. 1-3)
___
___
___

What happened on Jonah's voyage? (v. 4-9)
___
___
___

How did the mariners respond to the calming of the sea? (v. 10-16)
___
___

What did God do? (v. 17)
___
___

Day 3: Read Jonah 2

What was Jonah's attitude in his prayer? Give specific reasons for your answer. (v. 1-9)

What did God do? (v. 10)

Day 4: Read Jonah 3

What did Jonah do next? (v. 1-4)

What was the response of the king and the people to Jonah's message? (v. 5-9)

What did God do? (v. 10)

Day 5: Read Jonah 4

Why was Jonah angry? (v. 1-3)

How did God respond? (v. 4-8)

What was the lesson for Jonah? (v. 9-11)

Why do you think God ended the Jonah account like this?

For Further Study

Key Verses: "When my soul fainted within me, I remembered the Lord; and my prayer went up to You, into Your holy temple. Those who regard worthless idols forsake their own Mercy. But I will sacrifice to You with the voice of thanksgiving; I will pay what I have vowed. Salvation is of the Lord."

Jonah 2:7-9

Lesson 55

Overview

If you are able to study one of the many available timeline charts of the prophets (see Dr. Utley's www.freebiblecommentary.com and www.biblegateway.com for two good ones), you will notice a great deal of overlap in the timing of these writings. The chronology can be a bit challenging, but the messages of the prophets are both illuminating and inspiring for our own Christian journey. The prophets we are studying at this point are known as the pre-exilic prophets, showing that they prophesied before both Israel and Judah were taken captive by their enemies. We will study the captivity more in later lessons.

You may hear the prophecy books being categorized as "major prophets" and "minor prophets". These terms are not meant to be taken as "less important" or "more important". These terms simply refer to the length of the books. Most of the prophecy books are short (Obadiah, Joel, Jonah, etc.) while some are longer (Isaiah, Jeremiah, Ezekiel). The main issues we will be concerned with in our study are what messages the prophets had for the people of their day and what messages there are for us.

Isaiah gives the time of his writings in chapters 1 and 6 specifically. The challenge in Isaiah is that he mixes prophecies that would be fulfilled in the days of his writings with prophecies that have not yet been fulfilled 2,700 years later. But even though it takes careful study to distinguish the two layers of prophecies, Isaiah is rich with spiritual insights into so many aspects of our own relationship to God. We must always be careful of our tendency to "claim" certain Bible passages as universal promises of God for all of us. Many promises of God are applicable to all followers of God, while some are specific to a certain people, place and time. Take care to learn the difference.

Lesson 55

Daily Bible Study

Day 1: Read 2 Chronicles 26

What words/phrases describe Uzziah? (v. 1-5)

In what ways did Uzziah prosper? (v. 6-15)

How did Uzziah fall into sin? (v. 16)

What did the priests do? (v. 17-18)

What happened to Uzziah? (v. 19-23)

Day 2: Read Isaiah 1

Who were the kings of Judah during Isaiah's prophecies? (v. 1)

Who does God compare Judah to? (v. 2-11)

What specific things does God want His people to do? (v. 12-20)

Has Jerusalem been called the "faithful city" yet? (v. 21-26)

What specific things does God say about Jerusalem? (v. 21-31)

Day 3: Read Isaiah 2

Has this prophecy been fulfilled? (v. 1-4)

What does Isaiah want the Israelites forgiven for? (v. 5-9)

How is the "day of the Lord" described? (v. 10-18)

What kind of person are they to cut themselves off from? (v. 19-22)

Day 4: Read Isaiah 3

What exactly is God judging them for in this passage? (v. 1-12)

What does God condemn the leaders of Israel for? (v. 13-15)

What is their sin and its consequences here? (v. 16-26)

Day 5: Read Isaiah 4

What are the specific ways that God will restore Israel after His judgment on them? (v. 1-6)

For Further Study

Key Verse: " 'Come now, and let us reason together,' says the Lord, 'Though your sins are like scarlet, they shall be as white as snow; though they are red like crimson, they shall be as wool.' "

Isaiah 1:18

Lesson 56

Overview

We will continue to study the Kings/Chronicles accounts interspersed with the prophets, particularly Isaiah, for the next few lessons. We see more of the overlap in the chronology as we study further, and Isaiah gives us specific time periods for this section. These references are very helpful in sorting out the correct order for these writings.

Some days will have long chapters to study, while some of these chapters are much shorter. Use the days that have shorter chapters to review, compare and study more deeply on these great truths. Even the judgments that are for a particular group at a particular time have importance for our own spiritual growth. The sins that the people of that day and time committed are definitely worth our reflection and our prayer that we don't commit the same sins against God. Sometimes we form the habit of thinking that we would never commit certain sins such as idol-worship. But it is very good for us to consider what we put before God in our own lives, especially things that are representative of our culture like social media, academic or sports success, or even success in ministry. Even a singer for God can come to put more faith in his or her own talent and success than in singing for God's glory.

Another thought on ancient culture and pagan worship is that some of the most Godly kings in Judah sometimes had the most ungodly sons who ascended the throne immediately after them. And sometimes a very ungodly king produced a very Godly son as the next king. What happens spiritually from one generation to the next is definitely worth pondering. It is also good to keep in mind that Judah had some Godly kings and some ungodly kings, while all of the kings of Israel turned against God.

As always, study carefully to understand how to apply the specific truths of God that you are learning.

Lesson 56

Daily Bible Study

Day 1: Read Isaiah 5

What was the vineyard a symbol for, and what was God's complaint? (v. 1-7)

What was their primary sin? (v. 8-12)

What would be the consequences? (v. 13-17)

What are a few more specific sins of Israel? (v. 18-23)

What are a few more specific judgments? (v. 24-30)

Day 2: Read Isaiah 6

What stands out to you about Isaiah's encounter with God? (v. 1-5)

What mission did God give to Isaiah? (v. 6-10)

What will be left after God's judgment? (v. 11-13)

Day 3: Read 2 Chronicles 27

What was good and bad about Jotham's reign in Judah? (v. 1-9)
___
___

Day 4: Read 2 Chronicles 28   **(2 Kings 16)**

What specific sins did Ahaz commit? (v. 1-4)
___
___

What two kings defeated Judah and why? (v. 5-8)
___
___

What did Israel do with the captives from Judah? (v. 9-15)
___
___

What did Ahaz try to bribe the king of Assyria with? (v. 16-21)
___
___

Why did Ahaz worship idols, and what happened as a result? (v. 22-27)
___
___

Day 5: Read Isaiah 7

What was God's message through Isaiah to Ahaz? (v. 1-9)
___
___

What future prophecy did God give to Ahaz? (v. 10-16)
___
___

What more immediate prophecy for Ahaz and Judah is given? (v. 17-25)
___
___

For Further Study

Key Verse: "Also I heard the voice of the Lord, saying: 'Whom shall I send, and who will go for Us?' Then I said, 'Here am I! Send me.' "

Isaiah 6:8

Lesson 57

Overview

As we learned in lesson 56, Isaiah is not completely chronological in his prophecies. And as we have also mentioned, several prophets were prophesying in Israel and Judah during the same time period. God had special messages for His people then, as He does now, and He delivered those messages through many sources. There was no way for His people to claim they didn't know about God's message of judgment for disobedience and blessing for obedience. The same holds true today.

So even though we could study Amos, Hosea and Micah along with Isaiah, for continuity we will take each book by itself. We will still intersperse the history sections from Kings and Chronicles to remind us what was actually happening during the prophecies. Keep in mind that when a chapter is in parentheses beside the chapter we are studying, it means that the chapter in parenthesis has the same account. Try to read both if you can.

Isaiah uses a lot of symbols in his prophecies. For example, in chapter 8, the symbol of the "waters of Shiloah" stood for the provision of God for His people, which they refused. As you study, try to note the symbols and what they seem to stand for. Isaiah also gives us specific prophecies of the coming Messiah, as in chapter 9. It is helpful to note that Isaiah interspersed prophecies that would be fulfilled in their lifetime as well as prophecies for hundreds of years later, and even some that have not been fulfilled yet.

A helpful study tool for chronological study such as this is <u>The Narrated Bible in Chronological Order</u> (F. LaGard Smith, Harvest House, 1984). As we have mentioned, there is some debate over the exact dates of many of these prophetic books, but Dr. Smith's account is easy to read and keep the history of Israel in mind.

Lesson 57

Daily Bible Study

Day 1: Read Isaiah 8

What did the people refuse, and what would be the consequences? (v. 1-7)

_____
_____

Why would they be "broken in pieces"? (v. 8-10)

_____
_____

What specific instructions did God give to Isaiah? (v. 11-22)

_____
_____

Day 2: Read Isaiah 9

Who is this Promised One, and what is said about Him? (v. 1-7)

_____
_____

What does God say specifically about Israel's attitude? (v. 8-12)

_____
_____

What repeated statement in this chapter shows God's judgment on Israel? (v. 12-21)

_____
_____
_____

Day 3: Read Isaiah 10

Write any part of these specific prophecies that could be applied to our times. (v. 1-4)

_____
_____

What were the main sins of Assyria? (v. 5-19)

_____

What would be the result of these judgments on Israel? (v. 20-34)

___

Day 4: Read Isaiah 11

What parts of this prophecy have not been fulfilled yet? (v. 1-9)

___

Who is the "Root of Jesse" and how will His "banner" affect Israel? (v. 10-16)

___

Day 5: Read Isaiah 12

How can we know that Israel will ultimately accept Jesus as their Messiah? (v. 1-6)

___

(Use the extra time today to look up place names, as in a concordance, for deeper understanding of these powerful prophecies.)

___

For Further Study

Key Verses: "For unto us a Child is born, unto us a Son is given; and the government will be upon His shoulder. And His name will be called Wonderful, Counselor, Mighty God, Everlasting Father, Prince of Peace."

Isaiah 9:6

"Behold, God is my salvation, I will trust and not be afraid; for Yah, the Lord, is my strength and song; He also has become my salvation. Therefore with joy you will draw water from the wells of salvation."

Isaiah 12:2-3

Lesson 58

Overview

These chapters were surely a great encouragement to the faithful ones of Isaiah's day, as well as faithful believers today, that God will ultimately judge the enemies of His people. The judgments of God against His own people were meant to discipline them and teach them to fear the Lord their God. But the judgments against their enemies would insure their enemies' destruction. Sections of scripture like this one should encourage believers of this day and age about future events. We do not have to be anxious about "wars and rumors of wars", terrorist attacks, shortages of oil or any other calamities of our times. God has everything under His control, and He is not surprised by any world events.

In Isaiah 14 we have the first real history of Lucifer/Satan. We will learn more about his fall from grace when we get to Ezekiel. In this passage the king of Babylon is compared to Lucifer, while in Ezekiel it is the king of Tyre being compared. It would seem a very sober warning to a king to be compared to Satan. At this point in history, Babylon is still gaining power in the ancient world, although Assyria is still stronger.

We will read the brief account in 2 Kings 17 of Israel's fall to Assyria, which occurred in 722 B.C. This was not just another defeat in battle. This was the annihilation of Israel as a nation. In fact, Israel would not be recognized as a nation again until 1948. At this point in history the southern kingdom of Judah is still a nation, even though the northern kingdom of Israel has been completely destroyed. The reason for their destruction was their continued refusal to worship only God rather than the idols of their culture. Keep in mind that none of Israel's kings led the people in Godliness, but some of Judah's kings did lead the people well. This may be why God allowed Israel to face judgment so far ahead of Judah.

Lesson 58

Daily Bible Study

Day 1: Read Isaiah 13

How is the "day of the Lord" described? (v. 1-8)

Ultimately who will be punished? (v. 9-16)

What would God's judgment on Babylon look like? (v. 17-22)

Day 2: Read Isaiah 14

From what you know of world history, has this prophecy happened yet? (v. 1-2)

What further destructions did God put on Babylon? (v. 3-11)

Who is Lucifer, and what was his sin? Also, what is God's judgment on him? (v. 12-21)

What other enemies of Israel would be destroyed? (v. 22-32)

Day 3: Read Isaiah 17

What will be the results of God's judgments? (v. 1-8)

Give several specific reasons for God's judgments. (v. 9-14)

Day 4: Read Isaiah 19

What happens to Egypt? (v. 1-10)

Why will the Egyptians be afraid? (v. 11-17)

How will they be blessed? (v. 18-25)

Day 5: Read 2 Kings 17

What happened to Israel? (v. 1-6)

What specific reasons does God give for allowing His people to be completely defeated by the Assyrians? (v. 7-23)

Why did God send lions, and what did the king of Assyria do about it? (v. 24-28)

How did the people respond to God, and what did God tell them? (v. 29-41)

For Further Study

Key Verses: "But the Lord, who brought you up from the land of Egypt with great power and an outstretched arm, Him you shall fear, Him you shall worship, and to Him you shall offer sacrifice. And the statutes, the ordinances, the law, and the commandment which he wrote for you, you shall be careful to observe forever; you shall not fear other gods. And the covenant that I have made with you, you shall not forget, nor shall you fear other gods. But the Lord your God you shall fear; and He will deliver you from the hand of all your enemies."

2 Kings 17:36-39

Lesson 59

Overview

We will skip chapters 20-23 in our study. Again, this is for the sake of overview, and not because these chapters are less important. Try to find time to read them if you are able. Those chapters continue the specific judgments on specific groups of people, including Jerusalem and Babylon. As we read in the last lesson, Assyria had conquered Israel, and Babylon would soon conquer Assyria as well as Judah. Actually over one hundred years would separate the destruction of Israel (722 B.C.) and the destruction of Judah (586 B.C.). And a reminder: Israel would not be recognized as a sovereign nation again until 1948 (A.D.).

Keep in mind as you study Isaiah and the prophets that the reason God allowed them to be conquered was that they continually worshipped idols rather than God. We see over and over how God would deliver them if they showed the slightest inclination toward devotion to Him. But, as the cycle began in Judges, they would worship idols; God would take His hand of blessing away, and their enemies would defeat them. Then they would cry out to God for deliverance, and God would deliver them. For a time, they would enjoy fellowship with their loving heavenly Father, but soon they would turn back to the idols of their day. God allowed their ultimate destruction because they continually refused to worship only Him. It is interesting to note that the Jewish people never again worshipped idols, although we know they have not yet accepted Jesus as their Messiah.

Also to remember as you study: Isaiah and many other prophets contain promises that are applicable to all believers, but many of the prophecies are for specific people and times. It is important to be careful which scriptures you "claim" for yourself or for particular circumstances, as if God's promises can be applied haphazardly to any situation. Study prayerfully and carefully, and ask God to help you to learn the difference.

Lesson 59

Daily Bible Study

Day 1: Read Isaiah 24

Why specifically will God ultimately destroy the whole earth? (v. 1-6)

What will the ruined people do? (v. 7-15)

What will God do in the end? (v. 16-23)

Day 2: Read Isaiah 25

What are some of the blessings the Israelites could look forward to? (v. 1-5)

What other precious promises are given? (v. 6-9)

What will be brought down? (v. 10-12)

Day 3: Read Isaiah 26

What condition does God require for perfect peace? (v. 1-6)

How will people learn righteousness? (v. 7-9)

What will God ultimately do for Israel? (v. 10-15)

_____

Why should they hide themselves? (v. 16-21)

_____

Day 4: Read Isaiah 27

What further promises/prophecies are given to Israel? (v. 1-6)

_____
_____

What does God want destroyed? (v. 7-9)

_____

Who will worship and where? (v. 10-13)

_____

Day 5: Read Isaiah 28

Who turned out to be the "drunkards of Ephraim" and what happened to them? (v. 1-8)

_____

How are we instructed to learn? (v. 9-13)

_____
_____

How does God describe their efforts to satisfy themselves? (v. 14-20)

_____

How does Isaiah describe God? (v. 21-29)

_____
_____
_____

For Further Study

Key Verses: "You will keep him in perfect peace, whose mind is stayed on You, because he trusts in You. Trust in the Lord forever, for in Yah, the Lord, is everlasting strength."

Isaiah 26:3-4

Lesson 60

Overview

The writings of Isaiah are rich with imagery and very deep in meaning. Hopefully you are able to spend time as you read to appreciate the beautiful language of Isaiah. This section is written specifically for Jerusalem, but it has many lessons/applications for us as well. For example, in chapter 30 the Israelites are chastened for looking to Egypt for help in their times of trouble rather than turning to God. "Looking to Egypt" for them was trusting in military might or clever alliances with powerful nations. For us, "looking to Egypt" would mean anything we trusted in for deliverance other than God. We might decide that success for our lives is wrapped up in accomplishing certain worldly goals. Although having goals can be a good thing, we must always be sure our goals are in line with God's will for our lives. There are fine lines between doing our best for God's glory and doing our best for our own glory. Ask God to help you discern when you are depending on anything except Him for anything in life. Remember the phrase, "going down to Egypt" (or whatever the equivalent in your translation) means seeking help from any source besides God.

We will also begin the amazing story of Hezekiah, king of Judah. Interestingly, Hezekiah's story is told in detail in three different books: 2 Kings, 2 Chronicles, and Isaiah. There are eleven chapters devoted to Hezekiah's reign in Judah. Keep in mind that Israel had just been taken captive by Assyria, and Ahaz, Hezekiah's father and predecessor, was a very wicked king in Judah who led the people away from God. Hezekiah was a Godly king who wanted to bring the people back to true worship of God. Some of his story is found in all three books, so remember the chapters in parentheses will be the same account. Since 2 Chronicles gives more background to the beginning of his reign, we will begin there.

Lesson 60

Daily Bible Study

Day 1: Read Isaiah 29

Who do you think "Ariel" is? (v. 1-8)
___

What could you take as a warning here? (v. 9-13)
___
___

What further warning is given? (v. 14-16)
___
___

What will happen to the Israelites? (v 17-24)
___
___

Day 2: Read Isaiah 30

What did God pronounce judgment on here? (v. 1-5)
___
___

Why would anyone not want to hear the truth of God's Word? (v. 6-11)
___

Why was the Lord bringing judgment here? (v. 12-17)
___
___

Which of these prophecies/promises mean the most to you? (v. 18-26)
___
___

How would Assyria be judged? (v. 27-33)
___
___

Day 3: Read Isaiah 31

Why was it wrong for them to go to Egypt for help, and how do we sometimes make the same mistake? (v. 1-3)

_____
_____

What is God's ultimate plan for Jerusalem? (v. 4-5)

_____
_____

What is God's main goal for Israel? (v. 6-9)

_____
_____

Day 4: Read 2 Chronicles 29

What specific things did Hezekiah do in the first year of his reign? (v. 1-11)

_____
_____

How did the priests respond? (v. 12-19)

_____
_____

What is remarkable about their worship? (v. 20-30)

_____
_____

What additional details are given? (v. 31-36)

_____
_____

Day 5: Read 2 Chronicles 30

Why had they not kept the Passover before? (v. 1-3)

_____
_____

What message did Hezekiah send throughout Israel? (v. 4-9)

_____
_____

What was Hezekiah's prayer and God's answer? (v. 10-27)

_____
_____

For Further Study

Key Verses: "Therefore the Lord will wait, that He may be gracious to you; and therefore He will be exalted, that He may have mercy on you. For the Lord is a God of justice; blessed are all those who wait for Him."

Isaiah 30:18

"Your ears shall hear a word behind you, saying, 'This is the way, walk in it,' whenever you turn to the right hand or whenever you turn to the left."

Isaiah 30:21

Lesson 61

Overview

As we continue Hezekiah's story, you should notice the overlap in the different accounts. Just as it deepens our understanding of Jesus' life, ministry, and teaching to study all of the accounts in the gospels, so it deepens the spiritual truths of the Old Testament to study different accounts of the same events. Try to spend any extra time you have in reading all of the accounts. Hezekiah's life is particularly rich with spiritual truths for us even today. And it is interesting to notice how the accounts fit into the narratives of 2 Kings, 2 Chronicles and Isaiah.

2 Kings 18 gives us another look at the defeat of the Northern Kingdom, Israel. Keep in mind that the nation of Israel was split into the Northern Kingdom (Israel) and the Southern Kingdom (Judah) after Solomon's son and successor, Rehoboam, acted foolishly. So at the time we are now studying, Israel had been captured by Assyria, and the nation would not recover completely for 2,670 years. They were allowed to go back to their homeland during the time of the Persian Empire (we will study that a little later), but they were not a sovereign nation again until 1948.

The southern kingdom of Judah was still a functioning nation at this time. But the impact of Israel's defeat cannot be overstated. That is the reason that Hezekiah and his top men were so anxious about the threats from the Assyrians. As we all do, Hezekiah and the people of Judah learned a deeper level of trust as they saw God deliver them from the danger.

Study carefully to glean every lesson God has for you in the life of Hezekiah. His devotion to obedience and faith are inspiring. It is worth noting that, when Isaiah came to tell him he would soon die, he begged God to let him live longer, and during his extended life he managed to produce the most evil king Judah had ever known.

Lesson 61

Daily Bible Study

Day 1: Read 2 Kings 18 (Isaiah 36)

What did Hezekiah do to show his devotion and faith to God? (v. 1-6)

Why did Hezekiah give the king of Assyria all the gold? (v. 7-16)

What was the Assyrian king's message to Hezekiah? (v. 17-25)

Why did the Assyrian king's messengers continue to speak in Hebrew? (v. 26-37)

Day 2: Read Isaiah 37 (2 Kings 19)

What was Isaiah's response to Hezekiah's request? (v. 1-7)

What was Sennacherib's message? (v. 8-13)

What stands out to you in Hezekiah's prayer? (v. 14-20)

What was Isaiah's message? (v. 21-35)

What happened to Sennacherib? (v. 36-38)

Day 3: Read Isaiah 38 (2 Kings 20)

Why was Hezekiah upset? (v. 1-3)

What did God do? (v. 4-8)

What stands out to you in this prayer? (v. 9-22)

Day 4: Read Isaiah 39 (2 Kings 20 – again!)

What was Hezekiah's mistake and the consequence? (v. 1-8)

Day 5: Read 2 Chronicles 32

In this recap of events from Isaiah and 2 Kings, what further details do you notice? (v. 1-8)

What is the worst thing Sennacherib did? (v. 9-19)

What happened to Sennacherib and to Hezekiah? (v. 20-26)

How is Hezekiah remembered? (v. 27-33)

For Further Study

Key Verses: "Thus Hezekiah did throughout all Judah, and he did what was good and right and true before the Lord his God. And in every work that he began in the service of the house of God, in the law and in the commandment, to seek his God, he did it with all his heart. So he prospered."

2 Chronicles 31:20-21

Lesson 62

Overview

We will have to backtrack a bit at this point. Isaiah spans many years and the reigns of several kings, as do Amos, Micah and Hosea. In this lesson we will go back and pick up some prophecies that applied to the northern kingdom of Israel before their defeat and exile. We have already read in Kings and Chronicles about the fall of Israel to the Assyrians, so again, we are backtracking chronologically. The fall of Israel to the Assyrians happened in 722 B.C. Amos wrote around 760 B.C. – about 40 years before Assyria conquered Israel.

This lesson will be an overview of the book of Amos. Remember that these books are referred to as minor prophets because of the length of the books, not the importance of their messages. Because it takes a little more work to glean the spiritual truths in this portion of scripture, many people do not take the time to study the prophets, but there are rich blessings for the ones who are willing to invest in it.

Amos was an ordinary man, not of the priestly tribe of the Levites. He was not considered a "professional" prophet; in fact, he says he was a shepherd. He lived in the southern kingdom of Judah, but his prophecies were for the northern kingdom of Israel. He predicts the ultimate fall of Israel, so his message was not popular. He lets the people know that the judgment of the Lord is coming because of their disobedience and failure to love and serve the one true God. And just as people today do not like to think of the judgment of God, people back then did not want to hear it either. We all prefer not to think about the consequences of our own sins.

We will not study the entire nine chapters of Amos. These chapters will be representative of Amos' message. As always, try to find some time to read all of the chapters.

Lesson 62

Daily Bible Study

Day 1: Read Amos 1

What specific groups are being judged? (v. 1-5)
___
___

Why would these groups be judged? (v. 6-10)
___

Who is being judged and why, and what is the judgment? (v. 11-15)
___
___

Day 2: Read Amos 3

What do you learn about God's prophets and prophecies? (v. 1-8)
___
___

What are some specific punishments for Israel? (v. 9-15)
___
___

Day 3: Read Amos 4

What do you learn about the women of Samaria? (v. 1-5)
___
___

What was God doing and why? (v. 6-11)
___
___

What did God ultimately want? (v. 12-13)
___
___

Day 4: Read Amos 7

What did God do and what was Amos' response? (v. 1-3)

What were the visions and what did they mean? (v. 4-9)

What was Amaziah's response to Amos' prophecies? (v. 10-13)

What did Amos say would happen? (v. 14-17)

Day 5: Read Amos 9

What did God determine to do to Israel? (v. 1-4)

What does God remind Israel of? (v. 5-10)

What is God's ultimate will for Israel (after the judgments)? (v. 11-15)

* Remember: If you have any extra time this week, read the other chapters of Amos. Write any thoughts or lessons that you want to remember here.)

For Further Study

Key Verses: " 'I will bring back the captives of My people Israel; they shall build the waste cities and inhabit them; they shall plant vineyards and drink wine from them; they shall also make gardens and eat fruit from them. I will plant them in their land, and no longer shall they be pulled up from the land I have given them,' says the Lord your God."

Amos 9:14-15

Lesson 63

Overview

We are still backtracking a little chronologically. Micah and Hosea were also written during the time of Isaiah, Amos, and the last chapters of Kings and Chronicles. In the <u>Narrated Bible</u>, the individual chapters are put in chronological order, according to Dr. Smith. But rather than putting individual chapters in chronological order, we will do that with the books. Taking that approach, Amos, Hosea and Micah need to be studied during Isaiah's writings. So this lesson will focus on messages from Hosea and Micah that were written before Israel was overtaken by Assyria.

Even though much of these prophecy writings are repetitive, it is still very important to study all of them. Since God preserved these writings and gave them to us in the format that we have now in our Bibles, we should glean every spiritual lesson we can. Many Christians go their entire lives without studying or even reading these books because they are more difficult to understand.

The repetitive nature of these books shows how deeply God wanted to teach His people about true relationship with Him compared to the idol-worship of the unbelievers. He wants to teach us the same lesson today. As we read about Israel's and Judah's temptations to walk in the ways of the pagan nations, we must examine our ourselves and ponder what parts of our lives prevent us from being holy, as we are commanded. If we are to live holy lives, we must understand what tempts us away from that calling. For the Israelites, it was a desire to identify with their culture and worship idols. We must recognize that we have the potential to do the exact same thing. As we study the sins of ancient Israel, let's ask God to show us the things we do that break His heart. We must always choose to follow closely after His Word rather than be tempted away by a desire to identify with our culture.

Lesson 63

Daily Bible Study

Day 1: Read Micah 1

Who is being judged and why? (v. 1-7)

How would they show their shame? (v. 8-16)

Day 2: Read Micah 5

Who is God talking about, and what will He do? (v. 1-5)

How does God describe the strength He will give to Israel? (v. 6-9)

What are some specific sins God will take away from Israel? (v. 10-15)

Day 3: Read Hosea 1

Who did God tell Hosea to marry and why? (v. 1-2)

What did God tell Hosea to name his first son, and what did the name mean? (v. 3-5)

What was Hosea to name his daughter, and what did it mean? (v. 6-7)

What was Hosea's second son's name and its meaning? (v. 8-9)

What are some future promises for Israel? (v. 10-11)

Day 4: Read Hosea 6

What does Hosea urge the people to do? (v. 1-3)

Why is their faith compared to a morning cloud or dew? (v. 4)

What does God want from His people? (v. 5-6)

How does God describe His people? (v. 7-11)

Day 5: Read Hosea 14

What does God want Israel to do? (v. 1-3)

What do these images mean for Israel? (v. 4-7)

What would Israel ultimately learn? (v. 8-9)

For Further Study

Key Verses: "He has shown you, O man, what is good; and what does the Lord require of you but to do justly, to love mercy, and to walk humbly with your God?"

Micah 6:8

"Who is a God like You, pardoning iniquity and passing over the transgression of the remnant of His heritage? He does not retain His anger forever, because He delights in mercy. He will again have compassion on us, and will subdue our iniquities. You will cast all our sins into the depths of the sea."

Micah 7:18-19

"Afterward the children of Israel shall return and seek the Lord their God and David their king. They shall fear the Lord and His goodness in the latter days."

Hosea 3:5

"For I desire mercy and not sacrifice, and the knowledge of God more than burnt offerings."

Hosea 6:6

_____
_____
_____
_____
_____
_____
_____
_____
_____
_____
_____
_____
_____

Lesson 64

Overview

In this lesson we return to Isaiah, recognizing that he was prophesying several layers of future judgments and blessings for Israel. We begin in chapter 40 with verses that are quoted in the New Testament about John the Baptist. And even though John the Baptist is not mentioned by name in Isaiah, his message and ministry are described perfectly 700 years before he was born. Remember also that Isaiah was prophesying God's message of judgment that would happen in their lifetimes as well as the message of future redemption through His Son's first and second comings.

Keep in mind that God's chosen people, the Israelites, were set aside as the family and lineage of the Messiah, Savior of all. We can see that they were not chosen because they were particularly holy or obedient to God. God chose to protect and bless them to bring His only Son into the world in the flesh. We read in Matthew and Luke that both Mary and Joseph were descendants of Abraham through David. God chose to use Israel to show us what a true relationship with Him means. He wants everyone throughout history to understand the rich blessings of obedience and the severe consequences of disobedience. And this is why we study all of these accounts. It drives deep into our hearts the urgency of knowing God's commandments and being obedient to Him. We also recognize that we can read and study and still not obey the heart of God. Let us all do what James said: "Be doers of the word, and not hearers only, deceiving yourselves." (James 1:22)

Again, resist the temptation to apply every word of these prophecies to yourself. Some of the promises are obviously to all believers; some are meant specifically for Israel. Careful and prayerful study will help you to learn the difference. Many people never take the time to find out what particular verses mean, and they misunderstand God's message to us.

Lesson 64

Daily Bible Study

Day 1: Read Isaiah 40

What are some specific promises to Judah? (v. 1-5)

What does God say is eternal? (v. 6-8)

How would these words comfort God's people? (v. 9-14)

What are those who do not understand God's power tempted to do? (v. 15-20)

How can anyone "renew their strength"? (v. 21-31)

Day 2: Read Isaiah 41

What does God assure Israel of? (v. 1-13)

What will Israel ultimately understand, after all the judgments are accomplished? (v. 14-20)

What is God trying to say to His people? (v. 21-29)

Day 3: Read Isaiah 42

Who is the hope of Israel, and how will they acknowledge Him? (v. 1-9)

_____

What specifically would they be ashamed of? (v. 10-20)

_____

Why does God pour out His anger on His people? (v. 21-25)

_____

Day 4: Read Isaiah 43

What are the specific promises to Israel here? (v. 1-7)

_____

What promises do you notice are given often and in different ways? (v. 8-15)

_____

What offenses of Israel do notice are given often? (v. 16-28)

_____

Day 5: Read Isaiah 44

What does God want to be to Israel? (v. 1-8)

_____

What is the obvious flaw in idol-worship? (v. 9-20)

_____

What repeated promise is given to Israel? (v. 21-28)

_____

For Further Study

Key Verses: "The grass withers, the flower fades, but the word of our God stands forever."

Isaiah 40:8

"Have you not known? Have you not heard? The everlasting God the Lord, the Creator of the ends of the earth, neither faints nor is weary. His understanding is unsearchable. He gives power to the weak, and to those who have no might He increases strength. Even the youths shall faint and be weary, and the young men shall utterly fall, but those who wait on the Lord shall renew their strength; they shall mount up with wings like eagles, they shall run and not be weary, they shall walk and not faint."

Isaiah 40:28-31

"Fear not, for I am with you; be not dismayed, for I am your God. I will strengthen you, yes, I will help you, I will uphold you with My righteous right hand."

Isaiah 41:10

_____

_____

_____

_____

_____

_____

_____

_____

_____

_____

_____

_____

_____

_____

Lesson 65

Overview

As we continue the overview of Isaiah, try to read the chapters we are not including in our study. Keep in mind that every chapter is important and has a message for our hearts and minds. The chapters we are studying are representative of Isaiah's messages to Israel, to Judah, to their enemies, and to us as well, but read all the chapters if you have time. Many of the chapters we are studying are very short, so there will be extra time on some days to read more.

If you have cross references (other verses that may help explain a certain concept) in the margins of your Bible, try to take time to look up those extra verses. These can help you to connect the entire message of the Bible to the specific scriptures you are studying. If you do not have those references, try to find time to look up extra verses from a concordance, either a real book or an online concordance. It is very helpful to know, for example, that Cyrus (mentioned in chapter 45) was the king of the Persians who gave the order for the Israelites to return to their homeland after seventy years of captivity. We will read more about him in 2 Chronicles. The point is to be familiar with the people and places that Isaiah mentions in order to have greater understanding of his message. Remember that it is not appropriate to apply every promise of God in the Bible to ourselves. Some promises were meant for all of us, but some were meant for particular people at particular times. Ask the Lord to show you the difference as you study. It deepens our faith and our understanding of God and His dealings with us to prayerfully consider His Word this way.

Many verses of the last chapters of Isaiah are quoted and fulfilled in the New Testament. You will have the opportunity to look up some New Testament passages that will deepen your understanding of the life of Jesus.

Lesson 65

Daily Bible Study

Day 1: Read Isaiah 45

What is God's message to Cyrus? (v. 1-7)
_____
_____

What does God say about His own power and knowledge? (v. 8-13)
_____
_____

How does God encourage Israel? (v. 14-19)
_____
_____

What warnings does God give? (v. 20-25)
_____
_____

Day 2: Read Isaiah 53

Who exactly is Isaiah referring to? (v. 1-5; compare John 12:37-41)
_____
_____

How are we compared to sheep? How is Jesus compared? (v. 6-8)
_____
_____

What pleased God and gave Him satisfaction? (v. 9-12)
_____
_____

Day 3: Read Isaiah 55

What does God offer to His people? (v. 1-2; compare John 6:48-51)
_____

What is Israel's future? (v. 3-5)

How does God remind us of His power (omnipotence) and His knowledge (omniscience)? (v. 6-9)

What does God say about His Word? (v. 10-13)

Day 4: Read Isaiah 58

Why did the people complain, and how did God answer? (v. 1-5)

Describe the results of a true fast of God? (v. 6-12)

What further admonition does God give? (v. 13-14)

Day 5: Read Isaiah 61

Which of these word pictures encourages you the most? (v. 1-3; notice any New Testament quotes)

What specific promises does God give to Israel? (v. 4-7)

What does God hate? (v. 8-9)

What brings joy to Isaiah? (v 10-11)

For Further Study

Key Verses: "Remember the former things of old, for I am God, and there is no other; I am God, and there is none like Me, declaring the end from the beginning, and from ancient times things that are not yet done, say, "My counsel shall stand, and I will do all My pleasure."

Isaiah 46:9-10

"Seek the Lord while He may be found, call upon Him while He is near. Let the wicked forsake his way, and the unrighteous man his thoughts; let him return to the Lord, and He will have mercy on him; and to our God, for He will abundantly pardon. 'For my thoughts are not your thoughts, nor are your ways My ways,' says the Lord. 'For as the heavens are higher than the earth, so are My ways higher than your ways, and My thoughts than your thoughts."

Isaiah 55:6-9

Lesson 66

Overview

In this lesson we will conclude our study of Isaiah and press on with what was happening in Judah in 2 Kings and 2 Chronicles. We will also study an interesting chapter of Nahum, who was also prophesying during that time.

As we pick back up in Kings and Chronicles, remember that they are basically two accounts of the same events. We will answer questions from only one account, but the corresponding account is in parentheses, and it will be extremely helpful to your study to read both.

The Kings/Chronicles chapters begin with King Manasseh, Hezekiah's son. We remember Hezekiah as a good king of Judah. When Isaiah came to tell him that he was near the end of his life, he begged for more time. God gave him fifteen more years, and Manasseh was born during that time. Sadly, Manasseh brought much sin, heartache and judgment to Judah.

Next we turn to Nahum. Interestingly, his entire prophecy is about the destruction that would come to Nineveh for her wickedness. Think back to what you know about Nineveh. Remember Jonah? Jonah had been commanded to go to Nineveh about one hundred years before Nahum in order to offer them an opportunity to turn to God. Jonah did not want to offer them salvation, and he would obviously have preferred to be Nahum, prophesying their doom. The Ninevites of Jonah's day, including their king, did turn to God, but apparently the next generations turned away from God. So Nahum is commanded by God to foretell their destruction. An obvious lesson for us is that God has a plan and purpose for each of us, and we should be running toward it without complaint or resistance, no matter how much we would rather do something else.

Lesson 66
Daily Bible Study

Day 1: Read Isaiah 65

What specific sins did God point out? (v. 1-7)

___

What contrasts are given between God's servants and those who forsake Him? (v. 8-16)

___

Describe the new heavens and the new earth. (v. 17-25)

___

Day 2: Read 2 Chronicles 33   (2 Kings 21)

What are some of the wicked things that Manasseh did? (v. 1-9)

___

What happened to Manasseh? (v. 10-17)

___

What kind of king was Amon, and what happened to him? (v. 18-25)

___

Day 3: Read Nahum 1

What are some things we learn about God from these verses? (v. 1-5)

___

What happens to those who set themselves as enemies of God? (v. 6-11)

___

What is their final end? (v. 12-15)

Day 4: Read 2 Chronicles 34   (2 Kings 22)

How old was Josiah when he became king, and what are some of the things he did during his teen years? (v. 1-7)

What did Hilkiah find, and what was Josiah's response? (v. 8-21)

Who was Huldah, and what was her message? (v. 22-28)

What else did Josiah do? (v. 29-33)

Day 5: Read 2 Kings 23   (2 Chronicles 35)

How did Josiah restore true worship to Judah? (v. 1-8)

What were some specific sins of the previous leaders? (v. 9-15)

What two things did Josiah do next? (v 16-25)

Who were the next two kings, and how did they reign? (v. 26-37)

For Further Study

Key Verses: "The Lord is slow to anger and great in power, and will not at all acquit the wicked. The Lord has His way in the whirlwind and in the storm, and the clouds are the dust of His feet."

Nahum 1:3

"The Lord is good, a stronghold in the day of trouble; and He knows those who trust in Him."

Nahum 1:7

"Now before him [Josiah] there was no king like him, who turned to the Lord with all his heart, with all his soul, and with all his might, according to all the Law of Moses; nor after him did any arise like him."

2 Kings 23:25

Lesson 67

Overview

Both Jeremiah and Zephaniah were prophets during the time of King Josiah. Zephaniah and Josiah were related because Zephaniah was a great-great grandson of King Hezekiah, and Josiah was a great grandson. As we have mentioned, not many take the time to study these prophets and understand what was happening in Israel and Judah at the time of these writings. We are usually so eager to find how scripture applies to us personally that we miss the deeper truths revealed about God in His Word.

Zephaniah is a minor prophet, and his book has only three chapters. The first chapter is about judgment on Judah, which had been besieged by the Assyrians, but not yet completely defeated. Chapter two describes God's judgments on the nations that had oppressed His people. We learn that even if God allowed His people to be oppressed, there was still a harsh penalty for the ones who did it. Zephaniah ends with great words of hope for the future for God's people. We will study only 2 of the chapters, but read all three if you can.

Jeremiah is a major prophet; remember that major prophets and minor prophets are only referred to that way because of the length of the books, not the importance of their messages. Jeremiah's prophecies spanned the reigns of seven kings, from Manasseh to Zedekiah. Zedekiah was the last king of Judah before they were completely defeated. We will study Jeremiah in order of the chapters, even though most Bible scholars do not consider Jeremiah's prophecies to be chronological. Jeremiah shows us a lot of his feelings about the impending judgment on his people, and he tells us what was going on for him personally. Most of the people of Judah did not want to hear a message of judgment for their sins; they preferred false prophets who gave them pleasant messages rather than the truth of God. Prayerfully consider our tendency to do the same thing today.

Lesson 67

Daily Bible Study

Day 1: Read Zephaniah 1

How was Zephaniah connected to the royal line? (v. 1)

Who exactly will be cut off from the Lord and why? (v. 2-6)

What was significant about the king's children? (v. 7-8)

How did Zephaniah describe the judgment on Jerusalem? (v. 9-18)

Day 2: Read Zephaniah 3

What did God say about Jerusalem? (v. 1-7)

What about the faithful few? (v. 8-13)

What future blessings does God offer? (v. 14-20)

Day 3: Read Jeremiah 1

What was the time frame of Jeremiah's prophecies? (v. 1-3)

What was God's first message to Jeremiah? (v. 4-10)

What pictures did God give to Jeremiah, and what did they mean? (v. 11-16)

How did God instruct Jeremiah? (v. 17-19)

Day 4: Read Jeremiah 2

How did God begin His case against Israel? (v. 1-8)

What are the two evils, and what are the results? (v. 9-19)

How did God's people argue that they were obedient? (v. 20-28)

What did God say about their claim of innocence? (v. 29-37)

Day 5: Read Jeremiah 3

What did God compare to Israel? (v. 1-5)

What did God want them to do? (v. 6-13)

How did Jeremiah personally respond to God's pleas for Israel? (v. 14-25)

For Further Study

Key Verses: "The Lord is righteous in her midst, He will do no unrighteousness. Every morning He brings His justice to light; He never fails, but the unjust knows no shame."

Zephaniah 3:5

"The Lord your God in your midst, the Mighty One, will save; He will rejoice over you with gladness, He will quiet you with His love, He will rejoice over you with singing."

Zephaniah 3:17

"But the Lord said to me: 'Do not say, "I am a youth," for you shall go to all to whom I send you, and whatever I command you, you shall speak. Do not be afraid of their faces, for I am with you to deliver you,' says the Lord."

Jeremiah 1:7-8

Lesson 68

Overview

Jeremiah is a rich book to study, and that is partly due to how much of his heart and feelings he reveals. In fact, he is sometimes referred to as the "weeping prophet" because his writings contain so much personal emotion. And as we study Jeremiah, we certainly see that he experienced a lot of persecution because of his messages.

Also, keep in mind that reading all of the chapters is ideal even though we will study representative chapters. Sometimes the messages may seem repetitious, but you will get the full impact of what God wants to teach us by studying all of it. Use the extra lines in "For Further Study" to jot down notes about the chapters not specifically covered in this study. One obvious reason for God's repeating His message of judgment so often is to show that there was no way for the people then or for us today to misunderstand God's plan and purpose for us. He continually offers blessings for obedience and judgment for disobedience. And there is no way to miss that message.

One very important aspect of God's character that we see clearly in Jeremiah is how much His people's sins affect Him personally. Sometimes, especially in messages of judgment for sin, we might forget how deeply hurt God is by our sin. He knows that sin ruins us, and that the more we sin, the more damage we do to our own hearts. As our Creator God who desires a relationship with us, our sins hurt Him more than we can understand. Perhaps the closest we can come to comprehending His pain is to consider how painful it is for us to see people we love making choices that will ultimately hurt them. The disobedience and rebellion of the people broke Jeremiah's heart, and God's heart was broken too. Jeremiah's message also serves as an example that God did not necessarily mean our lives on earth to be easy; sometimes we will need to be reminded that the way of Christ is the way of the cross.

Lesson 68

Daily Bible Study

Day 1: Read Jeremiah 4

How does God offer hope to Israel and Judah? (v. 1-4)

Why did Jeremiah say God deceives His people? (v. 5-10)

What did God say was the worst part of their punishment? (v. 11-18)

How did Jeremiah express his feelings about God's judgment? (v. 19-31)

Day 2: Read Jeremiah 11

Does God reveal any new thoughts here? (v. 1-8)

Why did God tell Jeremiah not to pray for them? (v. 9-17)

Describe the conspiracy against Jeremiah. (v. 18-23)

Day 3: Read Jeremiah 12

What bothered Jeremiah? (v. 1-2)

What was God's warning? (v. 3-6)
___

What does God continue to offer? (v. 7-17)
___

Day 4: Read Jeremiah 13

Describe the symbol of the sash. (v. 1-11)
___
___

What does the wine symbolize? (v. 12-14)
___

Why did God question them? (v. 15-23)
___

What is surprising about this? (v. 24-27)
___
___

Day 5: Read Jeremiah 15

How did God emphasize His coming judgment? (v. 1-9)
___
___

How did Jeremiah express his sorrow? (v. 10-18)
___
___

How did God reassure Jeremiah? (v. 19-21)
___
___
___

For Further Study

Key Verses: "But this is what I commanded them, saying, 'Obey My voice, and I will be your God, and you shall be My people. And walk in all the ways that I have commanded you, that it may be well with you.' Yet they did not obey or incline their ear, but followed the counsels and the dictates of their evil hearts, and went backward and not forward."

Jeremiah 7:23-23

"Thus says the Lord: 'Let not the wise man glory in his wisdom, let not the mighty man glory in his might, nor let the rich man glory in his riches; but let him who glories glory in this, that he understands and knows Me, that I am the Lord, exercising lovingkindness, judgment, and righteousness in the earth. For in these I delight,' says the Lord.

Jeremiah 9:23-24

Lesson 69

Overview

One of the worst problems of Jeremiah's day was that the spiritual leaders of Israel and Judah were not presenting God's Word to the people; they were presenting their own twisted messages. Remember that the people of that day did not have their own personal copy of God's Word as we do. They had to depend on the priests and religious leaders to tell them God's Word. And those leaders were steering the people away from God. But notice that God always provides a way for His people to know and understand His message of truth and mercy. During this time, God's message was being given through Jeremiah.

It is good for us to notice how difficult Jeremiah's ministry was. We do not really see any relief for Jeremiah. He had an unpopular message of judgment from God that made the people and their leaders angry. But we also see words of hope for Israel's future blessing that would follow their return to God. One lesson for us is that our service to God may not always be enjoyable; we may have to do hard things, as Jeremiah did, in order to accomplish God's plan and purpose for us. We must all learn, as Jeremiah did, to obey God even when it is hard. True obedience comes when we are putting God's will above our own desires. A true follower of God has denied his or her own will. The phrase "take up his cross" (Matthew 16:24) means putting to death our own selfish ways.

We see throughout Israel's history how they resisted God's plan for them. From refusing to enter the Promised Land, to demanding a king like the other nations, to worshipping pagan idols, they continually went their own way. But before we judge them too harshly, let's examine our own hearts. If we are honest with ourselves, we can see how we often do the exact same thing.

Lesson 69

Daily Bible Study

Day 1: Read Jeremiah 17

Compare/contrast the cursed man and the blessed man. (v. 1-8)

How does Jeremiah describe our hearts? (v. 9-13)

How was Jeremiah's message received by the people? (v. 14-18)

What is important about the Sabbath? (v. 19-27)

Day 2: Read Jeremiah 18

What is the lesson of the potter? (v. 1-11)

How did the people respond? How did God respond? (v. 12-17)

How did Jeremiah respond? (v. 18-23)

Day 3: Read Jeremiah 19

Describe the details of this special message. (v. 1-9)

What was the point of this object lesson? (v. 10-15)

Day 4: Read Jeremiah 20

Who was Pashhur; what did he do, and what was God's response? (v. 1-6)

Why was Jeremiah so discouraged? (v. 7-10)

What comforted Jeremiah? (v. 11-13)

How does Jeremiah show his confused emotions? (v. 14-18)

Day 5: Read Jeremiah 23

What hope does God give the people? (v. 1-8)

What is the message about their prophets and priests? (v. 9-22)

What does God say about Himself? (v. 23-32)

What specifically would bring this perpetual shame to them? (v. 33-40)

For Further Study

Key Verses: "Blessed is the man who trusts in the Lord, and whose hope is the Lord. For he shall be like a tree planted by the waters, which spreads out its roots by the river, and will not fear when heat comes; but its leaf will be green and will not be anxious in the year of drought, nor will cease from yielding fruit."

Jeremiah 17:7-8

"The heart is deceitful above all things, and desperately wicked; who can know it? I, the Lord, search the heart, I test the mind, even to give every man according to his ways, according to the fruit of his doings."

Jeremiah 17:9-10

Lesson 70

Overview

Throughout the study of all of the books of prophecy, we see God promising blessings for obedience and judgment for disobedience. We see God allowing His own people to be plundered and destroyed by their enemies. We see God using ungodly nations to punish His people when they turn away from Him. But we also see God punishing the nations who treated His people badly. Think back to the beginning of Genesis 12 where we are first introduced to the idea that Abraham's family would become God's chosen people. Remember that God promised blessings for the people who treated the Israelites well and curses for those who treated them badly. We see many of those judgments in the study of the prophets and even throughout the study of history.

Even though God allowed these wicked nations to come against His people and to have victory over them, the wicked nations would be punished by God for doing it. God allowed the bad treatment but then punished the ones who did it. That is certainly a good lesson for our own Christian lives. Sometimes God allows difficulties in order to teach us to obey Him. Sometimes He even allows people to mistreat us to accomplish His will. But we do not have to worry about getting even with someone who hurts us. We can leave that to God, knowing that He will judge in righteousness all those who come against His people.

We read about specific false prophets who claimed to speak God's message, but who were prophesying lies to the people. We also see God's punishment on them. We might note that God's punishment for unconfessed sin is in His own time and not ours. Jeremiah likely had times in which he wanted to see God's judgment come sooner, especially on the false prophets. He very likely wondered why the ungodly seemed to prosper while he had so much suffering. Psalm 73 addresses this well.

Lesson 70

Daily Bible Study

Day 1: Read Jeremiah 24

Describe the time period of this message. (v. 1)
_____
_____

Describe the symbol of the "good figs"; can you name anyone this might apply to? (v. 2-7)
_____
_____

Who are the "bad figs", and what will happen to them? (v. 8-10)
_____
_____

Day 2: Read Jeremiah 25

Describe this time period. (v. 1)
_____
_____

What was the message? (v. 2-7)
_____
_____

What was the judgment/punishment, and how long would it last? (v. 8-14)
_____
_____

Describe God's judgment on the nations who would plunder His people. (v. 15-38)
_____
_____

Day 3: Read Jeremiah 26

Specifically who was Jeremiah speaking to, and what did he say? (v. 1-7)
_____

What was their response? (v. 8-11)

What was Jeremiah's further warning? (v. 12-15)

Who was Urijah, and what happened to him? Also, how was Jeremiah's life spared? (v. 16-24)

Day 4: Read Jeremiah 27

What did the bonds and yokes symbolize? (v. 1-10)

How would the people know who the false prophets were? (v. 11-18)

What would happen to the temple treasures? (v. 19-22)

Day 5: Read Jeremiah 28

Who was Hananiah, and what was his message? (v. 1-4)

What was Jeremiah's response? (v. 5-15)

What happened to Hananiah? (v. 16-17)

For Further Study

Key Verses: "For I will set My eyes on them for good, and I will bring them back to this land; I will build them and not pull them down, and I will plant them and not pluck them up. Then I will give them a heart to know Me, that I am the Lord; and they shall be My people, and I will be their God, for they shall return to Me with their whole heart."

Jeremiah 24:6-7

Lesson 71

Overview

Many famously quoted "coffee cup" verses are found in the book of Jeremiah. These are verses that are often used to decorate coffee cups or wall hangings. We notice when we look into the context of some of these verses that sometimes we have taken something to have a different meaning than what God intended. It is always important to understand what God was truly saying in His Word before we apply scripture haphazardly to every situation.

Jeremiah offers deep messages of hope for the future of Israel and Judah, even though he is having to deliver the messages of judgment for their sin. Chapter 31 has particularly hopeful words for God's people. As we study through Israel's future hope, we notice that a lot of the prophecies are still unfulfilled. The promise that they would be allowed to return to their land after 70 years was certainly fulfilled, but there are also passages about the Messiah that were fulfilled in the New Testament, long after Jeremiah prophesied. And there are passages for future hope for Israel that are still to be fulfilled. Chapter 33 fills in a lot of those details for us.

We won't study chapter 34, but it is an interesting passage about another sin that hasn't been specifically addressed. It was about their disobedience to God's laws concerning slaves. Slavery was first allowed for those who got themselves into debt and could not pay what they owed. They were expected to "sell" themselves for a certain amount of time to pay off their debts. Those were the days before credit cards, which still enslave people today. But the people were disobeying by not freeing their slaves in the manner God had commanded. Also, it is not the right conclusion from passages like this this that the Bible condones slavery. As we have studied idol-worship and breaking the Sabbath, God is showing us that we must not pick and choose our areas of obedience.

Lesson 71

Daily Bible Study

Day 1: Read Jeremiah 29

What two specific commands did God give His people? (v. 1-9)
___
___

How did God encourage them? (v. 10-14)
___
___

Who exactly is God punishing, and what is their punishment? (v. 15-23)
___
___

Who is Shemaiah; what did he do, and what was his punishment? (v. 24-32)
___
___

Day 2: Read Jeremiah 31

What are some specific words of hope and encouragement for Israel? (v. 1-14)
___
___

How did Ephraim respond to God's judgment? (v. 15-22)
___
___

What gave Jeremiah "sweet sleep"? (v. 23-30)
___
___

Describe the new covenant. (v. 31-40)
___
___

Day 3: Read Jeremiah 32

Why did Zedekiah put Jeremiah in prison? (v. 1-5)

Why did Jeremiah buy Hanamel's field? (v. 6-15)

What do you learn from Jeremiah's prayer? (v. 16-25)

How does this passage remind Jeremiah of God's plans for His people? (v. 26-44)

Day 4: Read Jeremiah 33

What is God emphasizing to Jeremiah? (v. 1-9)

What true King for Israel is God telling Jeremiah about? (v. 10-18)

What does God compare His covenant to? (v. 19-26)

Day 5: Read Jeremiah 35

How did the Rechabites demonstrate obedience? (v. 1-11)

How did God compare the obedience of the Rechabites to the obedience of His people? (v. 12-19)

For Further Study

Key Verses: "For I know the thoughts that I think toward you, says the Lord, thoughts of peace and not of evil, to give you a future and a hope. Then you will call upon Me and go and pray to Me, and I will listen to you. And you will seek Me and find Me, when you search for Me with all your heart."

Jeremiah 29:11-13

"Ah, Lord God! Behold, You have made the heavens and the earth by Your great power and outstretched arm. There is nothing too hard for You. You show lovingkindness to thousands, and repay the iniquity of the fathers into the bosom of their children after them-the Great, the mighty God, whose name is the Lord of hosts. You are great in counsel and mighty in power, for Your eyes are open to all the ways of the sons of men, to give everyone according to his ways and according to the fruit of his doings."

Jeremiah 32:17-19

"Call to Me, and I will answer you, and show you great and mighty things, which you do not know."

Jeremiah 33:3

Lesson 72

Overview

As Jeremiah 36 begins, Jehoiakim, son of Josiah, is king of Judah. This is an example of how Jeremiah's writings are not always chronological, even though we are studying them in numerical order. In chapter 35, Zedekiah was king, and he actually reigned after Jehoiakim. Chapters 36-37 show us why that happened.

Keep in mind that at this time in history the northern kingdom of Israel has been conquered and taken into captivity by the Assyrians. The Babylonians (also known as the Chaldeans) have come into power, overtaking the Assyrians and continually attacking Judah. These were days of tremendous upheaval as the strongest army of the day took over weaker nations and made them slaves.

As we have seen in our study of Jeremiah, he reveals more of his personal life than many of the other prophets. We know some things about Daniel, Jonah and Ezekiel as well, but most of the prophets do not tell us as much about the personal cost of their own prophecies. Clearly most of the messages of the prophets were for judgment on the people's disobedience, and messages like that are never popular. Sometimes the people responded with repentance; other times they responded with anger. In Jeremiah's case, there was some of both, but mainly he experienced negative responses from speaking out for God. In these chapters we see him put in prison and then in an even worse dungeon from which it took 30 men to pull him out. A big lesson for us is that doing God's will does not always bring good things for us in a worldly sense, but our eternal rewards are matchless.

Notice again that many of the passages meant to be encouraging to the Jews of that day can still encourage us today. Just continue to notice the context and avoid the temptation to apply scripture haphazardly.

Lesson 72
Daily Bible Study

Day 1: Read Jeremiah 36

What was the message of the scroll, and why did Baruch have to write it and read it? (v. 1-10)
___
___

How did the princes respond? (v. 11-19)
___
___

How did the king respond? (v. 20-26)
___
___

What did God have Jeremiah do? (v. 27-32)
___
___

Day 2: Read Jeremiah 37

Why was Zedekiah king, and what did Jeremiah tell him? (v. 1-10)
___
___

Why did Zedekiah secretly talk to Jeremiah, and what did Jeremiah tell him? (v. 11-21)
___
___

Day 3: Read Jeremiah 38

Why were the princes upset with Jeremiah? (v. 1-4)
___
___

What happened to Jeremiah, and who intervened for him? (v. 5-13)
___

What did Zedekiah really want? (v. 14-16)

What was Jeremiah's message? (v. 17-28)

Day 4: Read Jeremiah 39

What happened to Zedekiah, and why? (v. 1-10)

How were Jeremiah and Ebed-Melech spared? (v. 11-18)

Day 5: Read Jeremiah 40

Who was Nebuzaradan, and what choice did he offer Jeremiah? (v. 1-4)

What did Jeremiah choose? (v. 5-6)

What happened to the Jews who were left? (v. 7-12)

What warning did Gedaliah receive? (v. 13-16)

For Further Study

Key Verses: "But Jeremiah said, 'They shall not deliver you. Please, obey the voice of the Lord which I speak to you. So it shall be well with you, and your soul shall live."

Jeremiah 38:20

" 'But I will deliver you in that day,' says the Lord, 'and you shall not be given into the hand of the men of whom you are afraid. For I will surely deliver you, and you shall not fall by the sword; but your life shall be as a prize to you because you have put your trust in Me,' says the Lord."

Jeremiah 39:17-18

Lesson 73

Overview

In this lesson, Nebuchadnezzar has made a man named Gedaliah governor of Judah. In chapter 41 Gedaliah is murdered by a man named Ishmael. We meet Johanan in the same chapter, who comes to avenge the despicable acts of Ishmael. Johanan has a very admirable beginning as he rescues the Jews and vows to lead the people in obedience to God. He even seeks out Jeremiah to learn exactly what God wants them to do.

But Johanan does exactly what we often do: when he found out what God wanted them to do, it was not what he wanted, so he decided to go his own way. It is so easy when we are reading these accounts to think how crazy it was for them to disobey God like they did. But if our lives were written out, we would often look exactly like they did. We defend our disobedience in so many ways: "Surely God didn't mean that;" or "I'll forgive that person later;" and sometimes, "I'll serve God in that way at some other time."

God's will for them was to stay in Judah and serve Nebuchadnezzar in their own land. But they wanted to go to Egypt and hopefully escape Babylonian rule. "Going down to Egypt" has become a symbol in our study of doing our own will rather than God's will, or even trying to accomplish God's purposes in our own way rather than God's. Remember in Isaiah when the Israelites wanted to look to the Egyptian army, and God told them not to. Remember also in Exodus when the Israelites wanted to return to Egypt and slavery rather than following God's will into the Promised Land. Let it be a lesson to us not to "go down to Egypt" to help ourselves in our own way when God is leading us another way. We must always listen to and be obedient to God's will, even if it means sacrificing or denying our own will in order to obey and follow God's way - especially if it means denying our own will. That's the heart of following Jesus. (Matthew 16:24)

Lesson 73

Daily Bible Study

Day 1: Read Jeremiah 41

List all the sins of Ishmael. (v. 1-10)

Who was Johanan, and what did he do? (v. 11-18)

Day 2: Read Jeremiah 42

What did Johanan and all the people promise? (v. 1-6)

What were they forbidden to do? (v. 7-17)

What did Jeremiah accuse them of? (v. 18-22)

Day 3: Read Jeremiah 43

What did Johanan and the leaders say about Jeremiah's message? (v. 1-3)

What did they do? (v. 4-7)

What further message did God give to Jeremiah? (v. 8-13)

Day 4: Read Jeremiah 44

What did God say about the Jews in Egypt? (v. 1-10)

What excuses did the people give? (v. 11-19)

What would be their punishment? (v. 20-30)

Day 5: Read Jeremiah 45

How did Baruch feel about all that he had to write and see? (v. 1-3)

How did God encourage him? (v. 4-5)

*Since chapter 45 is so short, and we will not study chapters 46-51, this is a good time to look over those chapters and note what stands out to you about God's judgment on the nations.

For Further Study

Key Verses: "So they said to Jeremiah, 'Let the Lord be a true and faithful witness between us, if we do not do according to everything which the Lord your God sends us by you. Whether it is pleasing or displeasing, we will obey the voice of the Lord our God to whom we send you, that it may be well with us when we obey the voice of the Lord our God.' "

Jeremiah 42:5-6

" 'Do not be afraid of the king of Babylon, of whom you are afraid; do not be afraid of him,' says the Lord, 'for I am with you, to save you and deliver you from his hand. And I will show you mercy, that he may have mercy on you and cause you to return to your own land.' "

Jeremiah 42:11-12

Lesson 74

Overview

Before we finish the last chapter of Jeremiah, which reviews the fall of Jerusalem, we must stop and study the wonderful writings of Habakkuk. Habakkuk was writing his prophecies during the time of Jeremiah before Jerusalem was completely overthrown. We have seen in Jeremiah the horror of God's prophets as they realized that God's judgment was coming but the people still would not heed God's Word. Habakkuk is seen questioning God on His judgment, and we see God patiently explaining what He has been telling His people for centuries: blessings for obedience but curses and punishment for disobedience. And the punishment was coming quickly. After revealing his deepest emotions about God's punishment on Judah, Habakkuk ends with a beautiful picture of faith in God's goodness.

On Day 4 we will spend time studying the destruction of Jerusalem. It is helpful on many levels to spend time on this most historic moment in Jewish history. The account is given in detail in the four chapters listed, so if God wanted to describe this event in so many ways, we should definitely spend extra time considering all the lessons God has for us in it. You may want to spend the extra days this week contemplating the gravity of God's allowing the enemies of His people to destroy the temple, which was the symbol of His presence with them. He also allowed them to be carried away from the land that He had given to them. Remember He had promised that David would always have a son on the throne of Israel, but the kingdom of Israel comes to an end with this event. The promise of David's kingdom ultimately has its fulfillment in Jesus, who was called the Son of David. We see the earthly lineage of David to Jesus in Matthew 1 and Luke 3. It is interesting to note that in David's writings in the Psalms, many of the Psalms are known as "messianic" because they are about Jesus the Messiah.

Lesson 74

Daily Bible Study

Day 1: Read Habakkuk 1

What was Habakkuk's question to God? (v. 1-4)

What was God's answer? (v. 5-11)

What was Habakkuk's second question? (v. 12-17)

Day 2: Read Habakkuk 2

What did Habakkuk mean by this? (v. 1)

Who are the "just", and how do they live? (v. 2-4)

Who is being judged here? (v. 5-14)

What specific sins are mentioned? (v. 15-20)

Day 3: Read Habakkuk 3

What are some specific reasons for Habakkuk's praise? (v. 1-9)

What does Habakkuk ultimately accept as he prays? (v. 10-16)

How did Habakkuk respond to God's will? (v. 17-19)

Day 4: Read 2 Chronicles 36 (Jeremiah 52, 2 Kings 24, 25)

What happened to Jehoahaz? (v. 1-4)

What happened to Jehoiakim? (v. 5-8)

What happened during Zedekiah's reign? (v. 9-14)

How long did Jerusalem lay in waste? (v. 15-21)

Who was Cyrus, and what did he proclaim? (v. 22-23)

Day 5: Read Lamentations 1

What are some of the ways that Jeremiah describes Jerusalem's downfall? (v. 1-7)

What did Judah have to admit? (v. 8-14)

How did God's people feel? (v. 15-22)

For Further Study

Key Verses: "And the Lord God of their fathers sent warnings to them by His messengers, rising up early and sending them, because He had compassion on His people and on His dwelling place. But they mocked the messengers of God, despised His words, and scoffed at His prophets, until the wrath of the Lord arose against His people, till there was no remedy."

2 Chronicles 36:15-16

"Though the fig tree may not blossom, nor fruit be on the vines; though the labor of the olive may fail, and the fields yield no food; though the flock may be cut off from the fold, and there be no herd in the stalls-yet I will rejoice in the Lord, I will joy in the God of my salvation. The Lord God is my strength; He will make my feet like the deer's feet, and He will make me walk on my high hills."

Habakkuk 3:17-19

Lesson 75

Overview

As we ended Lesson 74 with the beginning of Lamentations, we will begin this lesson with the last chapter of Lamentations. Remember we are overviewing the Old Testament, so read every chapter if you can, using the two extra days each week.

Remember from Jeremiah's writings that he was put in a pit, kept in prison, and many other terrible things for doing exactly what God told him to do. A great lesson for us is that doing God's will does not always make us comfortable in this life. We are pilgrims in a foreign country, destined for a far better eternal home. We must always be willing to "deny ourselves, take up our cross daily, and follow Him" (Matthew 16:24). We must not look for a life of ease here on earth; we must be willing to do the hard things as Jeremiah did.

Next we will delve into the writings of Ezekiel. Ezekiel is the last of the major prophets. Remember that "major" and "minor" refer only to the lengths of the books. Again, this is an overview, so we will not study every chapter, but try to read the ones we skip. The chapters that we skip are no less important than the ones we read; we are just aiming for representative chapters. It will be a good idea to go back and study all the books of the Bible in more detail after you have laid the foundation of the message of the entire Bible.

Ezekiel has much more symbolism than we have studied so far. God uses many object lessons during this time to show His people exactly how His judgment would come. Ezekiel, like Jeremiah, was asked to do some very hard things for God, but he was also found obedient. Ezekiel, Daniel and Jeremiah all lived during the same time period, so try to keep that in mind as you study. Ezekiel is considered the easiest book to figure the dates because he mentions specific years and months.

Lesson 75
Daily Bible Study

Day 1: Read Lamentations 3

What are some of the ways that Jeremiah describes his despair over his situation? (v. 1-18)

___

How does Jeremiah describe God's faithfulness in adversity? (v. 19-27)

___

How are God's feelings described? (v. 28-33)

___

What does Jeremiah encourage himself and the people to do? (v. 34-42)

___

Why did Jeremiah cry? (v. 43-51)

___

What did Jeremiah want for the enemies of his people? (v. 52-66)

___

Day 2: Read Ezekiel 1

What are some of the details Ezekiel gives about himself? (v. 1-3)

___

What does Ezekiel seem to be describing? (v. 4-28)

___

Day 3: Read Ezekiel 2

After the astounding vision, what did Ezekiel hear? (v. 1-4)
_____
_____

What was God's first message to Ezekiel? (v. 5-10)
_____
_____

Day 4: Read Ezekiel 3

Why do you think God made Ezekiel eat the scroll? (v. 1-3)
_____
_____

How did Ezekiel feel about God's message? (v. 4-15)
_____
_____

What specific responsibilities did God give to Ezekiel? (v. 16-21)
_____
_____

What else did God instruct Ezekiel to do? (v. 22-27)
_____
_____

Day 5: Read Ezekiel 4

What did God command Ezekiel to do, and what did it symbolize? (v. 1-8)
_____
_____

What did the bread and water symbolize? (v. 9-17)
_____
_____

(*Note: You can go to most any health food store and find Ezekiel bread, made according to the recipe in Ezekiel 4:9, and there are many internet recipes too. It is considered a very healthy bread even today.)

For Further Study

Key Verses: "Through the Lord's mercies we are not consumed, because His compassions fail not. They are new every morning; great is Your faithfulness. 'The Lord is my portion,' says my soul, 'therefore I hope in Him!' The Lord is good to those who wait for Him, to the soul who seeks Him. It is good that one should hope and wait quietly for the salvation of the Lord."
Lamentations 3:22-24

"Then the hand of the Lord was upon me there, and He said to me, 'Arise, go out into the plain, and there I shall talk with you.' So I arose and went out into the plain, and behold, the glory of the Lord stood there, like the glory which I saw by the River Chebar; and I fell on my face."
Ezekiel 3:22-23

Lesson 76

Overview

We will skip chapters 5-11, but keep in mind they are not less important than the ones we will study. Try to use the extra days to study and take notes on the chapters we do not cover in this overview. Chapters 5-11 are full of more object lessons about the judgment God was bringing on Israel and Judah. The northern kingdom of Israel had already been destroyed by the Assyrians in 722 B.C. The southern kingdom of Judah, which was where Jerusalem and the temple were located, was destroyed by Babylon (who had defeated the Assyrians) in 586 B.C. Ezekiel was writing during the years from 593 B.C. to 571 B.C. Again, it is easy to date Ezekiel's writings because he gave us dates and kings.

Keep in mind that Jeremiah and Daniel were also contemporaries of Ezekiel. Daniel's writings, which we will study next, occurred in the years 605 B.C. to about 530 B.C. It is good to keep in mind the times of the writings of the prophets; it is also interesting to note that most historians generally agree with the time table of these world events.

As always, some of the chapters are very short (e.g. Ezekiel 14 and 15), while others are longer. If you need to pace yourself with dividing some of the longer chapters into more than one day and read parts of them on days with shorter chapters, that would work well.

As we study the colorful and dramatic writings of these prophets, try to imagine how they were feeling and what they were going through. Their times must have seemed devastating, yet God was revealing His plans to His prophets and His chosen people. And notice that God was always preserving a remnant to carry the family of Abraham, Isaac and Jacob all the way to the Messiah, specifically through the line of David, as He promised.

Lesson 76

Daily Bible Study

Day 1: Read Ezekiel 12

How did God show that He would hold back judgment if they repented? (v. 1-2)

What did God have Ezekiel do and why? (v. 3-7)

What did God repeatedly say was the reason for His judgment on His people? (v. 8-20)

What did the false prophets say, and what did God say? (v. 21-28)

Day 2: Read Ezekiel 14

Who exactly is before Ezekiel, and what does God say about them? (v. 1-5)

Where did God say their idols were, and what is the reason they will be punished? (v. 6-11)

Whom did God mention, and why? (v. 12-23)

Day 3: Read Ezekiel 15

What does God want them to know and why specifically would the land become desolate? (v. 1-8)

___

___

Day 4: Read Ezekiel 18

Why is the proverb false? (v. 1-4)

___

What is the main point here? (v. 5-9)

___

What are the two types of sons, and what will happen to them? (v. 10-17)

___

What was hard for them to understand? (v. 18-24)

___

What does God offer to every sinner? (v. 25-32)

___

Day 5: Read Ezekiel 20

What specific phrase does God use to describe Israel? (v. 1-6)

___

What was the purpose of the Sabbaths? (v. 7-12)

___

What specific sins were shared by the fathers and the sons? (v. 13-24)

___

How would they know that He is the Lord? (v. 25-38)

___

What was the purpose of the fire? (v. 39-49)

___

For Further Study

Key Verses: "Then I will give them one heart, and I will put a new spirit within them, and take the stony heart out of their flesh, and give them a heart of flesh, that they may walk in My statutes and keep My judgments and do them; and they shall be My people, and I will be their God."

Ezekiel 11:19-20

"I am the Lord your God; Walk in My statutes, keep My judgments, and do them; hallow My Sabbaths, and they will be a sign between Me and you, that you many know that I am the Lord your God."

Ezekiel 20:19-20

Lesson 77

Overview

In Ezekiel, God often says, "Then they shall know that I am the Lord." As you study, notice how often God repeats this thought. God said this to His own people as well as to the pagan nations that fell under His judgment. The judgments of God are meant to reveal to the people that God really is Who He says He is. God had held out grace and mercy for centuries, both to His people the Israelites and to the nations such as Assyria (remember Jonah?). But God's grace and mercy are never separated from His Truth, which is that we are created for fellowship with Him, and He does not have fellowship with darkness and sin. He even provides the atonement for that sin, so that all we have to do is look to Him. But even with such a simple task, we still often want to go our own way rather than God's way.

So as we study the sin of and judgment on the Israelites and the pagan nations, let us keep in mind how far short we also fall in obedience to God. But just as obedience would have prevented God's judgment in 586 B.C., obedience also prevents God's judgment in our lives today. All they had to do was to give their hearts to God, just as that is all we have to do today. And that means choosing a life of obedience to Him.

Here is another reminder to take notes, if possible, on the chapters that we do not include in our overview. It is interesting to note that chapters 29-32 are all full of God's specific judgments on Egypt. Try to think of all the reasons that God would spend so much time describing the calamities and even the ruin of Egypt after it had been a great and powerful nation for many centuries. A study of the nation of Egypt is interesting throughout their entire history. Also note that this lesson contains another description of Satan's fall from heaven, and Ezekiel's famous sermon to the dry bones.

Lesson 77

Daily Bible Study

Day 1: Read Ezekiel 28

How did the prince of Tyre feel about himself? (v. 1-5)

How did God feel about him? (v. 6-10)

To whom is God comparing the king of Tyre? (v. 11-19)

What promise is repeated to Israel? (v. 20-26)

Day 2: Read Ezekiel 33

What was the responsibility of the watchman? (v. 1-11)

What two things are said about "fairness"? (v. 12-20)

Describe again the reason for Judah's destruction. (v. 21-33)

Day 3: Read Ezekiel 34

Who were the shepherds? (v. 1-10)

In what specific ways does God describe Himself as their shepherd? (v. 11-22)

What further promises does God give to His people? (v. 23-31)

Day 4: Read Ezekiel 36

What did God say about the nations that plundered Israel? (v. 1-7)

What did God say about the land? (v. 8-15)

What did God say about Himself? (v. 16-23)

What are some further promises to Israel? (v. 24-38)

Day 5: Read Ezekiel 37

Describe the vision of the bones and what it meant. (v. 1-14)

Describe the two sticks and what they represented. (v. 15-22)

What two purposes would God's judgment and restoration of Israel show? (v. 23-28)

For Further Study

Key Verses: "So you, son of man: I have made you a watchman for the house of Israel; therefore you shall hear a word from My mouth and warn them for Me."

Ezekiel 33:7

"I will make them and the places all around My hill a blessing; and I will cause showers to come down in their season; there shall be showers of blessing."

Ezekiel 34:26

" 'I will raise up for them a garden of renown, and they shall no longer be consumed with hunger in the land, nor bear the shame of the Gentiles anymore. Thus they shall know that I, the Lord their God, am with them, and they, the house of Israel, are My people,' says the Lord God."

Ezekiel 34:29-30

"I will give you a new heart and put a new spirit within you; I will take the heart of stone out of your flesh and give you a heart of flesh. I will put My Spirit within you and cause you to walk in My statutes, and you will keep My judgments and do them."

Ezekiel 36:26-27

Lesson 78

Overview

In this lesson we will begin the fascinating and inspiring account of Daniel. Study the last chapters of Ezekiel as you have time, and take extra notes on the "For Further Study" page.

The last chapters of Ezekiel describe events that most scholars believe have not yet been fulfilled. If you study different commentaries and research these chapters, you will find many different interpretations. We must keep in mind that at least part of the reason God gave prophecy was to warn His people of impending judgment. Another reason was to give the ones who were truly trusting Him, as the prophets were, a future hope. Those two reasons are still important for us today. Another added benefit of the prophecies we have studied is to see the specific fulfillment of so many of them. It is of great benefit for us to study all of the Word of God, even the prophecies that might be very confusing. But it is not helpful to the body of Christ to develop dogmatic opinions of future events that will promote division rather than unity. We honor God by learning what He has told us, but keep in mind that at best "we see through a glass darkly" (1 Corinthians 13:12). There are some things we will not understand completely until we get to heaven, and as long as God is fine with that, we need to be fine with it too.

The book of Daniel is also full of prophecies that are still to come. But the beginning has immensely practical life lessons for all of us. Even if you are already familiar with the story of Daniel, you will be able to see how his life fits into the Old Testament timeline. Even though Daniel and his friends were taken from their homeland and forced to serve in Nebuchadnezzar's evil empire, they were faithful when faced with the choice to obey God or lose their lives. Daniel, Shadrach, Meshach and Abednego inspire us to courageously face harsh circumstances that challenge our commitment to Christ.

Lesson 78

Daily Bible Study

Day 1: Read Daniel 1

What kind of young men did Nebuchadnezzar want, and why? (v. 1-4)

What was offered to Daniel and his friends, and why did they refuse? (v. 5-8)

What did Daniel propose to Ashpenaz, and what was the result? (v. 9-16)

How are Daniel and his friends described? (v. 17-21)

Day 2: Read Daniel 2

What did Nebuchadnezzar demand? (v. 1-13)

What did Daniel do? (v. 14-23)

What did Daniel say about God? (v. 24-30)

What did the dream mean? (v. 31-45)

What happened to Daniel and his friends? (v. 46-49)

Day 3: Read Daniel 3

What did Nebuchadnezzar decree? (v. 1-7)

What was the response of Shadrach, Meshach and Abednego? (v. 8-18)

What happened to them? (v. 19-25)

What was Nebuchadnezzar's response? (v. 26-30)

Day 4: Read Daniel 4

Describe Nebuchadnezzar's second dream. (v. 1-18)

What did it mean? (v. 19-27)

What happened next, and how did Nebuchadnezzar respond? (v. 28-37)

Day 5: Read Daniel 5

Why was Belshazzar afraid? (v. 1-9)

What did the "handwriting on the wall" mean? (v. 10-31)

For Further Study

Key Verses: "Daniel answered and said: 'Blessed be the name of God forever and ever, for wisdom and might are His. And He changes the times and the seasons; He removes kings and raises up kings; He gives wisdom to the wise and knowledge to those who have understanding. He reveals deep and secret things; He knows what is in the darkness, and light swells with Him.' "

Daniel 2:20-22

"Shadrach, Meshach, and Abednego answered and said to the king, 'O Nebuchadnezzar, we have no need to answer you in this matter. If that is the case, our God whom we serve is able to deliver us from the burning fiery furnace, and He will deliver us from your hand, O king. But if not, let it be known to you, O king, that we do not serve your gods, nor will we worship the gold image which you have set up.' "

Daniel 3:16-18

Lesson 79

Overview

We already recognize and are blessed by the faith and perseverance of Daniel, Shadrach, Meshach and Abednego. We can apply great lessons to our own lives as we consider how these young men stood strong in obedience to God's Word, even in the face of persecution and death threats. Their lives prove that they were devoted to God. May we also be known for whole-hearted devotion to God.

This lesson begins with the famous story of Daniel in the lion's den. Nebuchadnezzar is no longer king; Belshazzar, who is named as a son of Nebuchadnezzar, has become king in chapter 5. Then in chapter 6, Darius the Mede has ascended the throne. It is worth noting that the Medes and Persians had united and overthrown the Babylonian empire, as Daniel's interpretation of Nebuchadnezzar's vision had shown. Darius also recognized Daniel's excellent character and leadership abilities and promoted him even higher in the kingdom. This promotion caused envy among the other officials, so plots were formed to get rid of Daniel. But God had other plans for him.

From chapter 7 through the end of the book (chapter 12), Daniel has visions and dreams of future times. As we mentioned in Ezekiel's prophecies, there is much disagreement among scholars about the exact interpretation of these prophecies. Even Daniel was not given the meanings. As we study these prophecies, it is good to remember that often God's people misunderstood how future events would unfold. Even in the New Testament fulfillment of the coming of Jesus the Messiah, the disciples did not understand the time difference between Jesus' first coming and His second coming. Keep studying the scripture in this way, and you will see how these prophecies align with history. It is very interesting to study all the different interpretations, and God blesses our devotion to His Word. Just be careful to let the Holy Spirit guide your thoughts.

Lesson 79

Daily Bible Study

Day 1: Read Daniel 6

Why was Daniel distinguished above Darius' other administrators? (v. 1-3)

What did the administrators propose to Darius, and why? (v. 4-9)

What did Darius do, and why? (v. 10-17)

What happened to Daniel? (v. 18-23)

What was Darius' response? (v. 24-28)

Day 2: Read Daniel 7

Briefly describe Daniel's dream. (v. 1-8)

What interesting details do you notice? (v. 9-14)

What was the interpretation of the dream? (v. 15-27)

How did the dream and the interpretation make Daniel feel? (v. 28)

Day 3: Read Daniel 8

Describe this vision. (v. 1-14)

How would Daniel understand the vision? (v. 15-18)

What was the interpretation? (v. 19-26)

What was Daniel's response? (v. 27)

Day 4: Read Daniel 9

What did Daniel understand, and what did he do? (v. 1-3)

Whose sin was Daniel praying over? (v. 4-11)

What did Daniel acknowledge about God's judgment? (v. 12-19)

Who spoke to Daniel, and what is the message? (v. 20-27)

Day 5: Read Daniel 10

Describe the vision and Daniel's response. (v. 1-9)

What was communicated to Daniel? (v. 10-21)

For Further Study

Key Verses: "At that time Michael shall stand up, the great prince who stands watch over the sons of your people; and there shall be a time of trouble, such as never was since there was a nation, even to that time.

"And at that time your people shall be delivered, every one who is found written in the book. And many of those who sleep in the dust of the earth shall awake, some to everlasting life, some to shame and everlasting contempt.

"Those who are wise shall shine like the brightness of the firmament, and those who turn many to righteousness like the stars forever and ever."

Daniel 12:1-3

Lesson 80

Overview

This lesson will conclude the book of Daniel and move into Ezra and Haggai. This is a time that it is interesting and helpful to keep the chronology straight in your mind. The events of Daniel spanned the years from about 605 B.C. through at least the 520's. We know that the fall of Jerusalem was 586 B.C., and Nebuchadnezzar likely took the young men, Daniel included, in 605 B.C. Since Darius is mentioned in Daniel, we know that the Daniel's time in Babylon lasted until at least the 520's since Darius' reign was from 522-486 B.C. It is helpful to our understanding of chronology that the writers included the Babylonian and Persian rulers, since we know the dates of their reigns.

Ezra begins where we left off in 2 Chronicles with the decree of Cyrus, king of Persia. Notice that Daniel did not mention Cyrus' reign. The first Persian king Daniel mentions is Darius, who is called a Mede. We know the Persian empire was also referred to as the Medo-Persian empire, so there is some debate over whether this was the same Darius. Cyrus' decree was given in 539 B.C., so Cyrus was king before Darius (although some believe they were the same person). Daniel would have been a very old man by that time, which may explain why he did not return to Jerusalem after Cyrus' decree that the Jews could return. Ezra tells the story of the first exiles returning to Jerusalem and beginning the rebuilding of the temple. Ezra himself did not return until 458 B.C. during the reign of Artaxerxes. Since the events of Esther happened during the reign of Ahasuersus, or Xerxes 1, that timeframe was between 486-464 B.C. So we see that after Daniel we must go back to Ezra, then insert Haggai, Zechariah, and Esther into that section of history to understand the order of events. As you study this section, ponder the question of why they did not all go back to their homeland when given the opportunity.

Lesson 80
Daily Bible Study

Day 1: Read Daniel 12

When does Michael stand up, and what is his message? (v. 1-4)
_____
_____

Who else is speaking, and what do they say? (v. 5-8)
_____

What is the final message recorded by Daniel? (v. 9-13)
_____
_____

Day 2: Read Ezra 1

Who was Cyrus, and what was his decree? (v. 1-4)
_____
_____

Who returned to Jerusalem, and what did they bring with them? (v. 5-11)
_____
_____

Day 3: Read Ezra 3

What did the returned captives do first? (v. 1-3)
_____
_____

What did they do next? (v. 4-7)
_____
_____

Why were some happy and some sad? (v. 8-13)

_____

_____

Day 4: Read Ezra 4

Who tried to discourage the rebuilding of the temple, and why? (v. 1-5)

_____

_____

How did they attempt to stop the rebuilding? (v. 6-16)

_____

_____

What was the king's response, and what was the result? (v. 17-24; notice what year this chapter ends with)

_____

_____

Day 5: Read Haggai 1

How did God describe their priorities, and what did He want them to do? (v. 1-11)

_____

_____

_____

What did the Israelites do? (v. 12-15)

_____

_____

_____

* Try to make a chart to show the chronology of this important time in Israel's history. Give the time period of each book we are studying.

_____

_____

_____

_____

For Further Study

Key Verses: "And they sang responsively, praising and giving thanks to the Lord: 'For He is good, For His mercy endures forever toward Israel.' Then all the people shouted with a great shout, when they praised the Lord, because the foundation of the house of the Lord was laid."

Ezra 3:11

"Now therefore, thus says the Lord of hosts: 'Consider your ways! You have sown much, and bring in little; you eat, but do not have enough; you drink, but you are not filled with drink; you clothe yourselves, but no one is warm; and he who earns wages, earns wages to put into a bag with holes.' Thus says the Lord of hosts: 'Consider your ways!'

Haggai 1:5-7

Lesson 81

Overview

Sorting out the chronology of Ezra and the books following it can be tricky. Keep in mind that Ezra begins with the years preceding the rebuilding of the temple when he had not yet come to Jerusalem. The decree was given that the Jews could return in 539 B.C. The first exiles returned and started rebuilding in 537 B.C. They faced a lot of opposition, and they actually stopped rebuilding for several years. God inspired Haggai and Zechariah to encourage them to continue the rebuilding of the temple.

It is interesting to note that Cyrus sent with the exiles all the temple treasures that Nebuchadnezzar took, but the Ark of the Covenant is not mentioned. Many of the gold and silver articles are accounted for, but there is no mention of the Ark. Through the centuries scholars have speculated about what may have happened to the symbol of God's mercy toward His people. Movies like Raiders of the Lost Ark spark interest in a possible dramatic archeological find, and there are many books and films about the possibilities. One of the more interesting theories is that the temple priests, knowing that Nebuchadnezzar's army was on the way to plunder Jerusalem, sent the Ark down to Egypt where it is still heavily guarded to this day. Some historians believe it may be found in one of the underground tunnels below Jerusalem. There is even speculation that the Ark was hidden beneath the city, and the actual blood of Jesus dripped through the earth to the mercy seat of the Ark. All of these are interesting to read and study, but God did not give us any more information about what happened to it.

Haggai and Zechariah give us their exact dates during the reign of Darius. As with so many of these prophecies, there are many different opinions about what they all mean. The visions of Zechariah are in this category. Since Zechariah has a number of short chapters, we will read two chapters on some of the days.

Lesson 81

Daily Bible Study

Day 1: Read Haggai 2

How did God encourage the ones who were sad about the new temple? (v. 1-9)

How were the people displeasing to God? (v. 10-14)

What did God want them to do? (v. 15-23)

Day 2: Read Zechariah 1

What was Zechariah's message, and how did the people respond? (v. 1-6)

Describe the vision and what it meant. (v. 7-17)

Describe the vision of the horns and what it meant. (v. 18-21)

Day 3: Read Zechariah 2-3

What was God's promise to Jerusalem? (2:1-5)

What further promises are given? (2:6-13)

What did God say to Satan? (3:1-2)

How did God encourage Joshua? (3:3-10)

Day 4: Read Zechariah 4 and 6

How did God encourage Zerubbabel? (4:1-7)

What further encouragement is given? (4:8-14)

Describe the vision of the horses. (6:1-8)

What was God's message to Joshua? (6:9-15)

Day 5: Read Zechariah 7

What did God say they did for themselves, and what should they have done? (v. 1-7)

What specific instructions were given, and what was the result? (v. 8-14)

For Further Study

Key Verses: " 'The glory of this latter temple shall be greater than the former,' says the Lord of hosts. 'And in this place I will give peace,' says the Lord of hosts."

Haggai 2:9

"So he answered and said to me: 'This is the word of the Lord to Zerubbabel: "Not by might nor by power, but by My Spirit," says the Lord of hosts.' "

Zechariah 4:6

_____
_____
_____
_____
_____
_____
_____
_____
_____
_____
_____
_____
_____
_____
_____
_____
_____
_____
_____

Lesson 82

Overview

In this lesson we will finish Zechariah, then pick back up chronologically in Ezra for two chapters. After that, the events of Esther begin. After Esther we will return to Ezra. Remember that the books with information about the kings are easier to date than the ones with no historical references. Also keep in mind that there is not complete agreement among scholars on the chronology of this section of history. Again, some scholars even believe that Cyrus and Darius may have been the same person. So don't give up if it seems too confusing. The main lessons for us are still evident, even if we disagree on the order of the events.

We will not study all of the chapters of Zechariah, but try to read all of them if you can. As we have mentioned, there is much debate over the meanings of some of his visions. Because all of the Bible is inspired by God and given to us for His reasons, we should try our best to understand every part of it. In every generation there are perilous world situations, and the study of prophecy helps us to remember that God has all nations and all world events in His hands. Even when we cannot understand why things happen the way they do, we can gain much peace in our hearts by studying how God has always worked in the lives of people and in the events of the whole world. Chapter 9 of Zechariah is plainly about the Messiah, so we are reminded that many of these visions were fulfilled in the New Testament.

We notice Haggai and Zechariah are mentioned in the next chapter of Ezra, and that certainly helps with order of events. So before we leave Ezra to study Esther, we see the temple completed after 16 years. Then after Ezra 6, the events of Esther unfold. It is interesting to consider how many of the Jews did not return to Israel when they were allowed to go back. Keep that in mind as you study; it is a biblically unanswered question that deserves consideration.

Lesson 82

Daily Bible Study

Day 1: Read Zechariah 8

What did God say about Jerusalem and the temple? (v. 1-10)

What further encouragement does God give to them? (v. 11-17)

What testimony do foreigners give? (v. 18-23)

Day 2: Read Zechariah 14

What clues are given about when these events occur? (v. 1-9)

What will ultimately happen to Jerusalem's enemies? (v. 10-15)

What points are made about the time of these prophecies? (v.16-21)

Day 3: Read Ezra 5

How were the Jews encouraged to continue building the temple? (v. 1-2)

Who tried to stop the building, and why were they unsuccessful? (v. 3-5)

Why did they send a letter to Darius? (v. 6-17)

Day 4: Read Ezra 6

What was Darius' response? (v. 1-12)

What happened next? (v. 13-14)

Describe the celebrations after the temple was completed. (v. 15-22)

Day 5: Read Esther 1

Why was Ahasuerus (Xerxes I) celebrating? (v. 1-4)

What did Ahasuerus want Vashti to do, and what did she do? (v. 5-12)

What did the king's advisors want him to do and why? Also, what did he do? (v. 13-22)

For Further Study

Key Verses: " 'And it shall come to pass that just as you were a curse among the nations, O house of Judah and house of Israel, so I will save you, and you shall be a blessing. Do not fear, let your hands be strong.' For thus says the Lord of hosts: 'Just as I determined to punish you when your fathers provoked me to wrath,' says the Lord of hosts, 'And I would not relent, so again in these days I am determined to do good to Jerusalem and to the house of Judah. Do not fear.' "

Zechariah 8:13-15

"Rejoice greatly O daughter of Zion! Shout, O daughter of Jerusalem! Behold, your King is coming to you; He is just and having salvation, Lowly and riding on a donkey, a colt, the foal of a donkey."

Zechariah 9:9

Lesson 83

Overview

The events of Esther occurred during the years from 483-473 B.C. We know this from the dates of the Persian rulers, and the ruler in the book of Esther is Ahasuerus, also known as Xerxes I.

Keep in mind that the Persian king Cyrus had decreed in 539 B.C. that the Jews could return to their homeland. He had also sent the temple treasures as well as everything they needed for their journey. The first group returned and laid the temple foundation in 537 B.C., but then opposition from their enemies caused the building to cease. We know men like Haggai and Zechariah were encouraging the building, but it still took about 16 more years before it was complete. The approximate time of completion was 520-516 B.C. More than 40 years later, we meet Mordecai and Esther. We will find out when we return to Ezra that Ezra himself returned to Israel during the reign of Ahasuerus. That's why we are reading Esther in the middle of Ezra.

It is interesting to consider why all the Israelites did not eagerly return to their homeland. Apparently the ones who did return lacked leadership and perseverance. Many of the ones who didn't return were surely too old to make such a long journey. And maybe they did not impress on the younger generations the importance and privilege of being able to return. We know that the sins of the nations of Israel and Judah caused God to allow them to be taken into captivity, so maybe many of them were not spiritually minded enough to feel an urgency to return. Did they know anything about the Word of God and His precise instructions for worship and sacrifice? Ezra had studied the Law, so we know it was available to some. Maybe they were so caught up in the culture of their time that it did not occur to most of them to want to go back. For whatever reasons, Mordecai and Esther stayed in Persia, and their presence there caused a lot of problems for the Jews who remained.

Lesson 83

Daily Bible Study

Day 1: Read Esther 2

What did the king's servants suggest? (v. 1-4)

What details are given about Mordecai? (v. 5-7)

What details are given about Esther? (v. 8-18)

What plot against the king did Mordecai discover? (v. 19-23)

Day 2: Read Esther 3

Who was Haman, and why was he angry? (v. 1-5)

What was Haman's plan? (v. 6-11)

Why was Shushan confused? (v. 12-15)

Day 3: Read Esther 4

Why were the Jews upset, and how did they show it? (v. 1-3)

What did Mordecai want Esther to do? (v. 4-8)

Why was Esther afraid, and what was Mordecai's response? (v. 9-14)

What did Esther do? (v. 15-17)

Day 4: Read Esther 5-6

Why do you think Esther put off her request for two days? (v. 1-8)

Why was Haman still angry, and what did he do? (v. 9-14)

Day 5: Read Esther 6

How is God's sovereignty shown in this situation? (v. 1-4)

Describe Haman's humiliation. (v. 5-12)

What did Zeresh say? (v. 13-14)

For Further Study

Key Verse: "For if you remain completely silent at this time, relief and deliverance will arise for the Jews from another place, but you and your father's house will perish. Yet who knows whether you have come to the kingdom for such a time as this?"

Esther 4:14

Lesson 84

Overview

In this lesson we will conclude the book of Esther, then return to Ezra where we left off. Remember that the events of Esther took place chronologically between Ezra 6 and 7.

An interesting feature of the book of Esther is that God is never mentioned. We see the sovereignty and the providence of God everywhere in the story, but we don't see the name of God. And although Mordecai is praised at the end of Esther as a man who was great among the Jews, one has to wonder whether he was great before God. He was one of the Jews who presumably could have returned to Jerusalem at any time during those years. But for some reason he chose to stay in the Persian capital city. The text shows us that he was second to the king in position by the end of Esther. But if he had been back in Jerusalem, where the Jews were supposed to be, the Jews in the kingdom of Persia would not have been in any danger; Haman would not have gotten angry and would likely have not desired to kill Mordecai's people. We do note that, even if Mordecai and Esther were in Persia due to unfaithfulness to God, God still preserved His people. It reminds us of Romans 8:28: "And we know that all things work together for good to those who love God, to those who are the called according to His purpose." The Bible never directly states that Mordecai and Esther were disobedient in not returning to Israel, but we know that Jerusalem was the place where the Jews were commanded to make sacrifices, so they were unable to worship God in the way God had commanded while they were in captivity.

About 20 years after the events of Esther, we see Ezra leaving Babylon and going to Jerusalem. Whatever the reasons for the delay, Ezra and Nehemiah did finally go back and help rebuild. Apparently their leadership was just what the exiles who returned needed. Ezra's knowledge of God's Word is noteworthy in this lesson.

Lesson 84

Daily Bible Study

Day 1: Read Esther 7-8

What happened to Haman? (7:1-10)

What happened to Mordecai? (8:1-2)

What was the next problem for the Jews, and what did the king propose? (8:3-8)

What was the solution, and how did the people respond? (8:9-17)

Day 2: Read Esther 9-10

What happened, and why? (9:1-5)

What happened to Haman's sons, and why? (9:6-14)

What was the Feast of Purim? (9:15-32)

How was Mordecai described? (10:1-3)

Day 3: Read Ezra 7

What details are given about Ezra? (v. 1-10)
_____

In what specific ways did Artaxerxes support Ezra? (v. 11-26)
_____

How did Ezra respond? (v. 27-28)
_____
_____

Day 4: Read Ezra 8

About how many men went with Ezra to Jerusalem? (v. 1-14)
_____

Who was missing; why was it important, and what did Ezra do? (v. 15-20)
_____
_____

Why did they fast? (v. 21-23)
_____

How did God answer their request? (v. 24-36)
_____
_____

Day 5: Read Ezra 9

What caused such grief for Ezra? (v. 1-4)
_____
_____

How did Ezra present the situation to God? (v. 5-15)
_____
_____
_____

For Further Study

Key Verses: "For Ezra had prepared his heart to seek the Law of the Lord, and to do it, and to teach statutes and ordinances in Israel."

Ezra 7:10

"Then I proclaimed a fast there at the river of Ahava, that we might humble ourselves before our God, to seek from Him the right way for us and our little ones and all our possessions. For I was ashamed to request of the king an escort of soldiers and horsemen to help us against the enemy on the road, because we had spoken to the king, saying, 'The hand of our God is upon all those for good who seek Him, but His power and His wrath are against all those who forsake Him.' So we fasted and entreated our God for this, and He answered our prayer."

Ezra 8:21-23

Lesson 85

Overview

Ezra concludes with the handling of an extremely touchy and controversial situation about mixed marriages - those in which one person is a follower of God and the other person is not. A major lesson for us is that absolute obedience is required. It is no good to say, "I love God," and then live however we choose or make up our own rules for living. The book of 1 John has quite a lot to say to us on that subject. The severity of the situation in Ezra 10 should have our attention as well.

Then we turn to Nehemiah. Nehemiah begins about 13 years after Ezra's return to Jerusalem. Once again, why did they not go back when they could? How did they justify being so comfortable in a pagan culture that they did not obey God and return to their homeland? As we have mentioned, many were surely too old to make the trip; perhaps their children and grandchildren did not understand the importance of the sacrificial laws. Somehow an urgency to return was missing in a large number of the exiles. Maybe some wanted to wait to see if the king's permission to return was really of God.

But at least Nehemiah was interested enough in his homeland to request permission from the king to return. Ezra had helped the people to reestablish their understanding of the Law of God. The temple was complete, but the walls of Jerusalem were still in ruins. It was not secure for cities back then not to be protected by a wall. So Nehemiah felt compelled by God to go back and rebuild the wall. In chapter one Nehemiah humbles himself and asks forgiveness for the people's sins, including his own. We notice that like Mordecai, Nehemiah had an established position of honor in the Persian kingdom. But he left Persia to return to Jerusalem to give much needed leadership to his people there. Nehemiah's commitment to the rebuilding of the wall and encouraging his people is a great example of persevering in service to God no matter what the obstacles.

Lesson 85

Daily Bible Study

Day 1: Read Ezra 10

What did Shechaniah propose? (v. 1-4)

_____

How did Ezra handle the situation? (v. 5-17)

_____

How did the men respond? (v. 18-44)

_____

Day 2: Read Nehemiah 1

Why was Nehemiah upset? (v. 1-4)

_____

Considering that almost 100 years had passed since the Jews were allowed back to Israel from their captivity, what was Nehemiah asking? (v. 5-11)

_____

Day 3: Read Nehemiah 2

What did the king notice? (v. 1-2)

_____

What was Nehemiah's response? (v. 3-5)

_____

What more did Nehemiah ask for, and how did he describe the king's response? (v. 6-8)

_____

How did Nehemiah approach the situation in Jerusalem? (v. 9-18)

___

Who was in opposition? (v. 19-20)

___

Day 4: Read Nehemiah 4

What was Sanballot's and Tobiah's response? (v. 1-3)

___

What did Nehemiah do? (v. 4-6)

___

How did Nehemiah respond to opposition? (v. 7-9)

___

How did Nehemiah encourage the Jews to keep building? (v. 10-15)

___

How did the people have to work? (v. 16-23)

___

Day 5: Read Nehemiah 5

What new opposition arose? (v. 1-5)

___

How did Nehemiah respond? How did the nobles respond? (v. 6-13)

___

What did Nehemiah do as governor of Judah, and why? (v. 14-19)

___

For Further Study

Key Verses: " 'O Lord, I pray, please let Your ear be attentive to the prayer of Your servant, and to the prayer of Your servants who desire to fear Your name; and let Your servant prosper this day, I pray, and grant him mercy in the sight of this man.' For I was the king's cupbearer."

Nehemiah 1:11

"And I told them of the hand of my God which had been good upon me, and also of the king's words that he had spoken to me. So they said, 'Let us rise up and build.' Then they set their hands to this good work."

Nehemiah 2:18

Lesson 86

Overview

Have you ever been so sure that God was leading you in a certain task or direction that nothing could stop you? That is exactly the kind of determination we see as we study Nehemiah's mission to rebuild the walls of Jerusalem. Nehemiah's account of the rebuilding of the wall should inspire each of us on multiple levels. Hopefully you will notice as you study passages like Nehemiah throughout your life that God will show you something new every time which will apply to your life at each stage.

One of the first things we notice in this week's lesson is Nehemiah's remarkable discernment of people and situations. How did he know when people were trying to trick him? That kind of wisdom comes only from God. In chapter 7 we see the names of the families that returned to Israel along with the number of members of each family.

In chapter 8 we see Ezra reading the Law of God to the people and their immediate desire to obey. Most of the people didn't have any idea how disobedient they had been since they did not have copies of the law, nor anyone to teach them while they were in captivity. So going back to Israel not only showed their desire for obedience, it gave them opportunities to learn and to practice greater obedience. That is how it always works: the more obedient we are, the more we want to obey. Let us never take for granted the opportunity we have been given to read and study God's Word for ourselves every single day.

Chapter 9 gives us a review of Israel's history. Chapters 10-12 are more numbers and genealogies. Chapter 13 concludes the book as Nehemiah returns to Israel and has to contend with the spiritual leaders who had led the people once again into sin against God. May we have the same boldness and zeal for holy living that Nehemiah had.

Lesson 86

Daily Bible Study

Day 1: Read Nehemiah 6

How did Nehemiah's enemies try to fool him, and how did he respond? (v. 1-4)

In what other ways did Nehemiah's enemies try to distract him, and how did he respond? (v. 5-14)

How long did it take to build the wall, and who got the credit? (v. 15-19)

Day 2: Read Nehemiah 8

What did Ezra do, and how did the people respond? (v. 1-5)

Why were the people grieving? (v. 6-12)

As they understood God's Word, what did they realize, and what did they do? (v. 13-18)

Day 3: Read Nehemiah 9

What actions of the people followed the reading of God's Word? (v. 1-3)

What were the leaders compelled to do? (v. 4-6)
_____

What did they say about Abraham? (v. 7-8)
_____

What did they say about Israel's captivity in Egypt? (v. 9-15)
_____

What was said about their time in the wilderness? (v. 16-21)
_____

What about their cycle of disobedience? (v. 22-31)
_____

After reviewing their history, what do they want to do? (v. 32-38)
_____
_____

Day 4: Read Nehemiah 10

Who was first to place his seal on the covenant? (v. 1-27)
_____

What did they commit to do? (v. 28-29)
_____
_____

Name some specific ways they obeyed God's Word. (v. 30-39)
_____
_____

Day 5: Read Nehemiah 13

In what 2 ways had the rulers sinned? (v. 1-14)
_____

What was another area of disobedience? (v. 15-22)
_____

How had they sinned in marriage, and what happened? (v. 23-31)
_____
_____

For Further Study

Key Verses: "They refused to obey, and they were not mindful of Your wonders that You did among them. But they hardened their necks, and in their rebellion they appointed a leader to return to their bondage. But You are God, ready to pardon, gracious and merciful, slow to anger, abundant in kindness, and did not forsake them."

Nehemiah 9:17

"But after they had rest, they again did evil before You. Therefore You left them in the hand of their enemies, so that they had dominion over them; yet when they returned and cried out to You, You heard from heaven; and many times You delivered them according to Your mercies."

Nehemiah 9:28

Lesson 87

Overview

We come to the last book of the Old Testament, Malachi. It is also the last of the history books of the Old Testament. We still have the poetry/worship section to study, so it's not the end of our study yet. Malachi is one of those books about which historians debate the exact chronology. But as you read and study, you will see that Malachi is actually a timeless book that applies to our relationship with God in every age. As we have seen in the Old Testament as a whole, obedience to God in action and attitude are emphasized. As you study, you will see how the message of Malachi could fit with a number of times in the history of Israel.

We have studied the nation of Israel, God's chosen people, since Genesis. We have seen their triumphs and their tragedies. We have wondered how they could seemingly so easily get caught up with the sins of their culture. As you have studied, hopefully you are able to see that the way the Israelites lived in the Promised Land is exactly comparable to our own Christian lives. All of the study of the history of Israel should be lesson after lesson for us about the exact way we should follow God: in perfect communion that grows directly from the roots of obedience. In these lessons we have repeatedly seen the blessings for obedience and judgement for disobedience. Let us apply those same principles to our own lives.

The last reading for this lesson will be a review of where we have been with the nation of Israel. This review is found in the Jewish hymnbook we know as the book of Psalms. Most of the Psalms were written by King David, but some were written by others throughout the kingdom years. One Psalm was written by Moses many centuries before this time, and some Psalms we are unsure who the author was. We will have the opportunity to study more of Psalms in the next few lessons.

Lesson 87

Daily Bible Study

Day 1: Read Malachi 1

What is God's first contention with His people, and how does He prove His point? (vv. 1-5)

_____

_____

What is God's second contention against them, and what details does He give about it? (vv. 6-14)

_____

_____

Day 2: Read Malachi 2

What is this addressing, and what is God's warning? (vv. 1-2)

_____

Who is Levi, and what did God say about him? (vv. 3-6)

_____

What had the priests done? (vv. 7-9)

_____

What was Judah's offense? (vv. 10-12)

_____

What was the second thing? (vv. 13-17)

_____

_____

Day 3: Read Malachi 3

What will the messenger do, and is more than one messenger implied? (vv. 1-3)

_____

_____

What was the main thing they would be judged for? (vv. 4-7)

___

How had they robbed God, and how would God bless them if they obeyed? (vv. 8-12)

___

How would they know the difference between the righteous and the wicked, and how does the difference matter? (vv. 13-18)

___

Day 4: Read Malachi 4

What will happen on the coming day? (v. 1)

___

What is promised to those who fear the name of God? (vv. 2-3)

___

What two men of God are mentioned and why? (vv. 4-6)

___

Day 5: Read Psalm 106

What was the result of the Red Sea miracle? (vv. 1-12)

___

Name several specific sins of the people. (vv. 13-27)

___

In what other ways did they sin, and what was the result? (vv. 28-48)

___

For Further Study

Key Verses: "For I am the Lord, I do not change; Therefore you are not consumed, O sons of Jacob."

Malachi 3:6

"Then you shall again discern between the righteous and the wicked, between one who serves God and one who does not serve Him."

Malachi 3:18

"They soon forgot His works; they did not wait for His counsel, but lusted exceedingly in the wilderness, and tested God in the desert. And He gave them their request, but sent leanness into their soul."

Psalm 106:13-15

Lesson 88

Overview

We have finished the history section of the Old Testament, and now we will study the section known as the poetry books. Traditionally these books are Job, Psalms, Proverbs, Ecclesiastes, and Song of Solomon. We have already studied Job, located historically during Genesis, so we will conclude the Old Testament study with the other four poetry books.

Rather than studying chronologically, we will first study King Solomon's writings in Ecclesiastes and Song of Solomon. The reason for taking these books out of order is that we will use the study of Psalms and Proverbs to transition to a different type of study in which you will not need a book like this to continue your personal study.

Song of Solomon was apparently written earlier in Solomon's life, so we will study it before Ecclesiastes. There are many interpretations for the Song of Solomon. Some scholars point out the beauty of the love God created between a husband and wife. Some compare it to the relationship of God and Israel, as in Hosea. Some compare it to Christ and the church, as in Ephesians 5. These comparisons may run into challenges because of Solomon's ungodly view of marriage (1 Kings 11).

This would be a good time to review what you have studied about the life of Solomon, which is found in 2 Chronicles 1-9 and 1 Kings 1-11. 1 Kings 11 tells the sad story of how Solomon turned away from God, even after God had blessed him with wisdom and great wealth. Ecclesiastes is Solomon's summation of his ungodly quest for the meaning of life. The key concept in Ecclesiastes is vanity, or emptiness. Solomon spends a lot of time describing how no earthly pleasures can ultimately give contentment. Of course he concludes with the great truth that nothing matters except to "fear God and keep His commandments" (Ecclesiastes 12:13).

Lesson 88
Daily Bible Study

Day 1: Read Song of Solomon 3

(As always, try to read the chapters that we skip as you have time.) Why did the Shulamite want to bring her lover to her mother's home? (vv. 1-5)

_____

_____

How did she describe Solomon? (vv. 6-11)

_____

_____

Day 2: Read Song of Solomon 6

How do you know from this passage that the Shulamite is not Solomon's only wife? (vv. 1-8)

_____

_____

How did Solomon describe her? (vv. 9-13)

_____

_____

Day 3: Read Ecclesiastes 1

What did Solomon call himself, and what are his initial observations? (vv. 1-8)

_____

_____

What did he emphasize next? (vv. 9-11)

_____

_____

What was discouraging to Solomon? (vv. 12-18)

_____

_____

Day 4: Read Ecclesiastes 2

What was Solomon searching for? (vv. 1-11)

_____

_____

Why did he become more discouraged? (vv. 12-17)

_____

_____

How did Solomon explain earthly accomplishments? (vv. 18-26)

_____

_____

Day 5: Read Ecclesiastes 3

How could these verses bring hope? (vv. 1-8)

_____

_____

What encouraged Solomon? (vv. 9-15)

_____

_____

What did he conclude about the righteous and the wicked? (vv. 16-22)

_____

_____

* Since these readings were comparatively shorter, spend some time studying the other chapters of Song of Solomon and Ecclesiastes, and write any further lessons you learn. You might even spend some time in 2 Chronicles 1-9 and 1 Kings 1-11 pondering what happened to Solomon.

_____

_____

_____

_____

_____

_____

_____

For Further Study

Key Verses: "Set me as a seal upon your heart, as a seal upon your arm; for love is as strong as death, jealousy as cruel as the grave; its flames are flames of fire, a most vehement flame. Many waters cannot quench love, nor can the floods drown it. If a man would give for love all the wealth of his house, it would be utterly despised."

Song of Solomon 8:6-7

"Let us hear the conclusion of the whole matter: Fear God and keep His commandments, for this is man's all. For God will bring every work into judgment, including every secret thing, whether good or evil."

Ecclesiastes 12:13-14

Lesson 89

Overview

As promised, these last two lessons will help you transition to personal study without this book as a guide. We will use Psalms and Proverbs to develop a different type of study from this point.

In Psalms and Proverbs, we see the practical application of the two greatest commands: "Jesus said to him, 'You shall love the Lord your God with all your heart, with all your soul, and with all your mind. This is the first and great commandment. And the second is like it: "You shall love your neighbor as yourself." On these two commandments hang all the Law and the Prophets.' " (Matthew 22:37-40)

On this basis, the daily study of Psalms and Proverbs can help each of us as we seek to obey these two greatest commands of God. Psalms is the collection of songs and hymns that the Jews have used for all these centuries in praise and worship of God. Many of the Psalms are the deepest heartfelt feelings of the writers (mostly David) as they poured out their thoughts to God. Some of them are quite startling as they ask God to bring severe punishments on their enemies. A very important thing to notice is that the Psalmists brought every thought and feeling to God. At the end, they always ended up with God's perspective of earthly situations. That is a critical lesson in prayer for us: we bring everything to God in prayer, and He helps us learn to trust Him and walk more closely with Him.

Billy Graham, the famous evangelist, reads 5 Psalms and 1 chapter of Proverbs each day. With that schedule, he reads the entire books of Psalms and Proverbs every month. Many others have patterned their daily Bible study after this. Dr. Graham reads in order: day 1: Psalms 1-5; Proverbs 1; day 2: Psalms 6-10; Proverbs 2, and so on. Another suggestion is to read according to the date. For example, on the 5th of the month, read Psalms 5 and Proverbs 5. As you get used to reading these books, add more chapters until you are reading 5 Psalms and 1 Proverb each day. Adding 30 is a convenient way to keep track: for example, on the 5th day of the month, read Psalms 5, 35, 65, 95 and 125. Some days you may have time for one; some days all five. The important thing is daily time in God's Word.

So in this lesson, begin choosing one Psalm each day. Then write any verse that stands out to you, or other thoughts you might offer to God from that day's reading. Next week we will do the same with Proverbs.

Lesson 89
Daily Bible Study

Day 1: Read Psalm _____

_____
_____
_____
_____
_____

Day 2: Read Psalm _____

_____
_____
_____
_____
_____

Day 3: Read Psalm _____

_____
_____
_____
_____

Day 4: Read Psalm _____

_____
_____
_____
_____
_____

Day 5: Read Psalm _____

_____
_____
_____
_____
_____

Day 6: Read Psalm _____

_____
_____
_____
_____
_____

Day 7: Read Psalm _____

_____
_____
_____
_____
_____

*Notice there are 7 days of readings now. Since the 5-day pattern of the previous lessons was to provide the opportunity to have a couple of days per week to catch up, it is now a good time to transition to be sure you are spending daily time in God's Word. You also won't necessarily need a page "For Further Study" since these are based on your own notes/verses in every chapter.

Lesson 90

Overview

If reading and meditating on the Psalms helps us learn to pray and relate to God better, then reading and meditating on the Proverbs can help us to have better relationships with our fellow humans. Keep in mind that King David wrote most of the Psalms, and King Solomon, David's son, wrote most of the Proverbs. We have already studied Solomon's writings in the Song of Solomon and Ecclesiastes. Now we will turn our attention to the collection of Proverbs that have been inspired and preserved by God.

There are many facets to this amazing portion of scripture. One thing to notice is the emphasis on Godly wisdom. Godly wisdom is contrasted with earthly foolishness throughout the book. Another important emphasis is on avoiding fools. This is a point that must be pondered carefully as we consider that Jesus said, "...whoever says, 'You fool!' shall be in danger of hell fire." (Matthew 5:22) And we are also instructed to "Judge not, that you be not judged." (Matthew 7:1) So if Proverbs spends a fair amount of space describing fools and foolish behavior that we are to avoid, how are we to resolve this with Jesus' words? First of all, you can recognize that someone is a fool without calling that person a fool. And the word for "judge" from Matthew 7 is better translated, "condemn". We are instructed in Proverbs to recognize fools and avoid them, and then Jesus told us not to condemn them for their foolish ways.

Again, it is a good practice to try to read a chapter of Proverbs every day. The lessons we learn here are so important and practical for our everyday lives. And reading according to the date (for example, on the 5th of the month, read Proverbs 5) is a good way to keep track. So choose the Proverbs you want to read, and write any verses or thoughts that stand out. Notice that space is provided to include a chapter of Psalms each day as well.

Lesson 90

Daily Bible Study

Day 1: Read Proverbs _____

Psalm _____

Day 2: Read Proverbs _____

Psalm _____

Day 3: Read Proverbs _____

Psalm _____

Day 4: Read Proverbs _____

Psalm _____

_____
_____
_____

Day 5: Read Proverbs _____

_____
_____
_____

Psalm _____

_____
_____
_____

Day 6: Read Proverbs _____

_____
_____
_____

Psalm _____

_____
_____
_____

Day 7: Read Proverbs _____

_____
_____
_____

Psalm _____

_____
_____
_____

So What Now?

Hopefully you have received multiplied blessings for completing this entire overview of the Old Testament. Hopefully your love of the study of God's Word has grown, and you realize how lost we are in our Christian lives without it.

This book was designed to show you a way to study and take notes for maximum understanding. The questions were meant to teach you to draw out a specific truth from each passage. Then in the last two lessons you were able to practice doing that on your own, without guided questions. Now you will be able to practice this process on your own. The study of the Bible is unlike any other book study; repeatedly studying the same lessons gives us new insights as we mature in Christ.

If you have enjoyed this study, you may want to get a copy of New Testament 101, also available at www.amazon.com. In the New Testament study, you will read and study all of the chapters of the New Testament in chronological order. It is a great blessing to study through the entire Bible and have the whole revelation of God in your heart. Then you can go back and study individual books with greater understanding.

The next step is to get a blank notebook in which to take notes. There are many successful ways to study God's Word, and it is a great investment of time to figure out which way is most effective for your personal growth. A blank notebook will provide space to take notes on your further reading and study of the Bible. Date your readings and record what chapter(s) you read. Then take notes on what God is saying to you and record verses that stand out. If you have questions about a particular passage, be sure to find a Bible study mentor who can discuss confusing passages with you. As mentioned in the introduction, www.biblos.com is also an excellent resource.

Some people find that they always learn more from a guided study. If you find that a guided study is more helpful for you, there are many good ones on the market today. You could search websites like www.christianbooks.com, www.creativebiblestudy.com, or the Bible app on your phone or computer. Just be sure not to fall into the destructive habit of studying more about what certain authors say about the Bible than the Bible itself. Be sure the focus is always on God's Word.

Again, New Testament 101 is a good next step in your study for now. God bless you as you continue to learn of Him through the study of His Word.

In Christ,

Jodi Green

"For the Word of God is living and powerful, and sharper than any two-edged sword, piercing even to the division of soul and spirit, and of joints and marrow, and is a discerner of the thoughts and intents of the heart." (Hebrews 4:12)

Study Helps:

The Believers Study Bible: New King James Version, Thomas Nelson, Inc., 1991

The Narrated Bible in Chronological Order, F. LaGard Smith, Harvest House, 1984

The Bible Knowledge Commentary, John F. Walvoord and Roy B. Zuck, Victor Books, 1988

Thru The Bible with J. Vernon McGee, J. Vernon McGee, Thomas Nelson Publishers, 1982

www.biblos.com

www.freebiblecommentary.com

www.creativebiblestudy.com

www.icr.org

www.answersingenesis.org

www.creationtoday.org

Made in the USA
San Bernardino, CA
28 August 2017